Fire in the Rain

liber geographicus pro bono publico

FIRE IN THE RAIN

The Democratic Consequences of Chernobyl

Peter Gould

The Johns Hopkins University Press
BALTIMORE

First published 1990 by
The Johns Hopkins University Press
701 West 40th Street
Baltimore, Maryland 21211

All photographs in this book are reproduced by kind permission of the author.

Library of Congress Cataloging-in-Publication Data
Gould, Peter, 1932–
    Fire in the rain: the democratic consequences of Chernobyl /
Peter Gould.
        p. cm.
    Includes bibliographical references.
    ISBN 0–8018–4052–X
    1. Radioactive pollution — Europe.   2. Chernobyl Nuclear Accident.
Chernobyl, Ukraine, 1986 — Environmental aspects — Europe.
I. Title.
TD196.R3G68   1990
363.17'99'09457714—dc20   89–77061 CIP

For Kate, Dick, and Andrew

Contents

Acknowledgements

No book like this, cutting across a score or more of fields, could possibly have been written without the generous help of many others. Among those who helped in one way or another, I would like to thank Gunhild Beckman, Gunnar Bengtsson, Ronny Bergman, Noel Broadbent, Gösta Carlestam, Helen Couclelis, Michael Cullingford, Kjäll Danell, Lars Emmelin, Gärd Folkesdotter, Olle Findahl, Per-Torsten and Margareta Fjällgren, Christopher Flavin, Torgny Frembeck, Robert Gale, Miles Goldstick, Roger Granlund, Ulf Grimås, Tor Gunnerød, Christopher and Ann Hohenemser, Staffan Holmgren, Brenda Howard, Torsten and Britt Hägerstrand, Zbigniew Jaworowski, Thomas Johansson, Malin Jonsdotter, Robert Kates, Anna Knowles, Lars Lander, Lars Gunnar Larsson, Joyce Lee, Lawrence Lidsky, Sally Lilienthal, Leif Moberg, Lennart Olofsson, Gunnar Olsson, Mats Olsson, Harry Otway, Ingar Palmlund, Robert Petersen, Jan Raihle, Dagmar Reichert, Josef Stark, Joseph Strahl, Wladyslaw Strumillo, Sören Svensson, Torgen Westermark, Goran Wickman, Ingrid, Thure, Thomas and Eilert Åhrén, Sture Öberg. Special thanks to Lori Friday for all the typing.

They may not agree at every point with what I have written, and for this reason I take sole responsibility. But whether agreeing or disagreeing, I do hope they feel the questions are worth pursuing.

The author and publisher are grateful to Penguin Books and Andrew Nurnberg Associates for permission to reproduce extracts from *Sarcophagus: A Tragedy* by Vladimir Gubaryev, translated by Michael Glenny (Penguin Books, 1987), copyright © Vladimir Gubaryev, 1986, this translation copyright © Michael Glenny, 1987, p. 63, pp. 66–7.

Peter Gould
State College, Pennsylvania
May 1989

Preface: Connecting things up

We live today in an intellectually fragmented world. You can see the first quiver of disconnection starting in the seventeenth century, as questions probing nature began to hive off from a core of philosophical concern more than two millennia old. It was not long before they congealed into the formal and specialized inquiries that we now call the "physical sciences." Natural philosophy dissolved, and physics and chemistry came into being. As they focused more sharply on the world of material things they generated yet more specialized fields, peopled by men and women who found it increasingly difficult to articulate their findings even to each other.

We now know that these developments were only the vanguard of modernity. In the eighteenth century, the sciences of the living world also started to separate out from the intellectual flux, catalyzed by an age of exploration that disclosed a myriad of life forms never suspected before. As these new disciplines entered and shaped the university, they too were split into ever-more sharp, penetrating, and specialized fragments. Brittle shards are razor sharp, and to dissect nature you have to keep on breaking them to keep the edges keen. In the nineteenth century, the sciences of the human world followed in what now appears to be a natural and inevitable sequence. Political economy settled out of a once holistic and morally informed inquiry about the human condition, only to break into a politics and an economics where moral questions are shunted aside as matters too embarrassing to mention. The rest is split between sociology's concern for the modern literate society, and anthropology's concern for traditional and preliterate forms. The process of intellectual fission continues, and it cannot be otherwise. The day when one person could grasp the known world has long since past.

But two disciplines, with a dogged, "dammit all" tenacity, still harbor within them an antifragmentary, moving-against-the-tide tradition that is felt in the bones, rather than justified by convoluted explanation. They are geography and history, the "sciences," the fields of knowing, of human space and time. Like shepherds of the intellectual world, their practitioners insist on rounding up the strays, on taking the fragmented pieces of the physical, living, and human worlds, and bringing them back together in place and period. And often, like good shepherds, they help each other out, for the best know that history without place and space is empty, and geography without period and time is static and sterile. Not that they are free themselves from the fissioning process of specialization, but many still feel it is a curse about which they can do little. The explosion of historical and geographical knowledge since the nineteenth century ensures that no one can grasp more than a fraction of either. But the tradition of synthesis, while often denigrated as superficial, is still honored on occasion, and has never been needed more than in today's fractured global landscape, with its disconnected, almost lobotomized sense of historical time. For this geographer it is one of two traditions in his discipline that inform this book.

The other is the equally old and informing geographic concern for relations between the physical, living, and human worlds, relations that are so assiduously torn apart by the partitional thinking to which we are so carefully conditioned – until drought, acid rain, ground water pollution, tropical forest clearance, disease vectors, ozone holes, industrial filth, population pressures, desertification, lifeless lakes and rivers . . . until we are reminded sharply that we are an integral part of our planetary home. If the bell tolls for us today it is because we are pulling the rope of our own death knell. Do not misunderstand me: this is no claim for geography's exclusive concern for relationships between the physical and living environments and the human presence, for these are so fraught with complexity that only specialized research in many fields, and along many fronts, can illuminate them. But geography's concern for the conjoining of the physical and human worlds was a tradition of inquiry guarded while others snoozed, a tradition flowering once again as we all try to create a more humane and decent environment for all living things on this earth, the only home we have.

These are the informing strands of the geographical heritage – a tradition of synthesis connecting things together in real spaces and places, and a traditional concern for human and environmental relationships. And then Chernobyl exploded. An event of the physical world, caused by the human, and rebounding back on the living world, lay squarely in that human–environmental cleft where things have to be brought together in order to understand what is really going on. The effects of that explosion travelled far in geographic space, and will be with us for generations in historical time.

Today, in modern medicine, radioisotopes are used in minute quantities as tracers to disclose invisible structures within the human body – brain tumors, clogged arteries, connections and obstructions of all sorts. In some strange but similar way, the radioactive fallout from Chernobyl has also served as a tracer, moving through the physical and living worlds to disclose their chains of connection. It has also crossed over those connections to reveal some startling things about the structures of the bodies politic in all their bureaucratic power. In neither case – real fallout moving through living structures, or figurative fallout moving on political structures – are the effects healthy or reassuring. Both living bodies and bodies politic are capable of developing malignancies. The fallout of Chernobyl disclosed not only grave problems for human health, but equally grave problems for democracies relying increasingly upon bureaucratized government informed by industrial and scientific power. In neither case is the story a pretty or commendable one as we trace it across the structures connecting the physical, living, and all-too-human worlds together. To the degree that we can keep these intact in our thinking, and refuse to defuse the issues by disconnecting and partitioning them in traditional ways, so a larger understanding can inform and strengthen democratic society itself.

You may think this is a large claim, but see what you think at the end. For the moment, join me in the spring of 1986 in the Ukraine.

1 A Ukranian spring

There were still patches of snow on the ground at Chernobyl that late April weekend, but you could see the sun rising higher in the sky each day. It would not be long now before its warmth melted the last bits of snow and ice, helped by the warm winds from the Crimea and the Black Sea. Then the buds would burst forth once again to clothe the trees in bright leaf, and the dark, rich earth of the Ukraine would put on its mantle of green once more. Song birds were already returning from their long winter migrations, and as rivers and streams unlocked themselves from the winter's ice, fishermen looked to their rods and tackle. Grateful for the warmth on stiff joints, old and kerchiefed women smiled and gossiped over stalls of vegetables at market, lingering under the bright spring sun and clear blue skies. Children came out into the sunshine and played once again those age-old games that pass so tenaciously and mysteriously from one generation to another.

At the power station, with its four huge reactors, the day shift went home, leaving behind the reduced night-time staff to watch over the atomic furnaces, great stark symbols of the modern age. From out of the heart of the atom they produced much of the electricity for the Ukraine, with its old cities of Kiev and Kharkov, its towns and villages and homes, its factories and collective farms. There was to be some sort of safety test that Friday evening, something the electrical engineers wanted to carry out. It had been done before, both at Chernobyl and at other similar reactors around the country. In fact the engineers had already started reducing the power level in Reactor 4 during the early hours of Friday morning, winding it down to half its normal output by early afternoon. Then an unexpected surge of demand for electricity had delayed the test, but it would probably be better to conduct it late at night anyway, when most people were asleep and less power was needed. After all, you had to have these safety tests, although everyone knew that an accident was so close to impossible that no rational person, no person who knew the slightest thing about science, believed that one could really happen. With all the safety features and procedures in place, with all our knowledge of science and engineering technology, experts had computed that there was only one chance in a hundred thousand – maybe even one in 10 million –

that anything really serious could happen. You took a greater risk when you crossed the street or smoked a single cigarette. It was quite absurd to worry.

At 1 hour, 23 minutes, and 43 seconds after midnight on April 26, 1986, Reactor 4 at Chernobyl went into a soaring and uncontrolled chain reaction. Two seconds later the resulting steam explosion tore the concrete housing apart, blew the thousand ton "safety" cover off the top of the reactor, and spewed radioactive materials high into the night sky equal to all the atomic tests ever conducted above ground.

What happened at Chernobyl?

2   A scientific and technical excursion

To understand what happened in those early morning hours at Chernobyl we shall have to make an excursion into atomic engineering, with a short but necessary digression into atomic physics, the science that underpins all the nuclear engineering applications. The reactor that exploded at Chernobyl was a relatively simple, even rough and ready boiling water pressurized tube reactor, the name describing quite accurately its basic features. Water is pumped under pressure through tubes, heated to a boiling water–steam mixture, which is then used in quite conventional ways to turn turbines producing electrical power. But underneath this rather bland description there is considerable technical complexity, for the heating source is atomic fission that has to be carefully controlled within very narrow and sensitive limits. Let us see exactly what is involved.

The heart of the Chernobyl reactor consisted of 2,000 tons of graphite blocks shaped into a massive cylinder about 7 meters (23 feet) high and 12 meters (38 feet) across. Graphite is a pure and rather soft form of carbon, and stiffened with a mixture of clay it is familiar to us as the "lead" in our pencils. It is a common and relatively cheap material, and has the property of absorbing or slowing down bits of atoms called neutrons, an ability that becomes very important, as we shall see in a minute.

Inserted into the massive block of graphite were 1,680 tubes spaced 25 centimeters (9.8 inches) apart, half of them serving a set of turbine generators on one side, half powering a second, identical set on the other. The tubes were made of pure zirconium alloyed with a small amount of niobium, both rather rare and relatively expensive metals, but necessary because they have a high resistance to corrosion under extreme temperatures and pressures. They are often used in making the turbine blades that run white hot in jet engines. In an atomic reactor, pressures and temperatures can be equally extreme. Temperatures inside the fuel rods can rise to 2,100° C (3,812° F), and to prevent everything from melting 37,600 tons of water are pumped through each hour at pressures of 6.8 mega pascals (MPa) (nearly 1,000 pounds per square inch).

The fuel for the reactor was 190 tons of uranium oxide (UO_2), "packaged" or clad in tubes also made from a zirconium–niobium alloy.

And it is here that we have to make our digression into atomic physics before we can understand exactly how energy is created to make electrical power or lethal explosions. Our digression will probably horrify a professional physicist or chemist for simplifying physical processes that are extremely complex. But it has taken many first-rate people in these fields more than a century to clarify such complexity, and the research still goes on today. We can only hope to understand a few basic facts that all this effort has established, but these should be enough for our purposes.

When we think of an atom, we usually picture a minute amount of matter with a dense core or nucleus of protons and neutrons bound together at the center, surrounded by electrons orbiting the nucleus equal to the number of protons – rather like planets swirling around the sun. In the nucleus, protons are rather massive particles with a positive electrical charge, while neutrons have almost no mass and a neutral (thus "neutron") charge. Surrounding the dense core of the nucleus are rings or shells of electrons each with a small negative charge, and a mass of only 1/1,836th of the heavy protons at the center. All matter is made up of these three basic building blocks, and depending upon how many protons, neutrons and electrons there are, we recognize different elements – oxygen, carbon, chromium, uranium, and so on.

In actual fact, when we talk about "matter" and "elements" in our everyday language, we tend to be rather sloppy as far as a physicist or a chemist is concerned. This is because an element (like carbon), with an equal number of protons and electrons, can appear in slightly different forms (for example, carbon 12 and carbon 14), depending on the number of neutrons sharing the nucleus with the protons. These various forms are called nuclides, and some are quite stable (carbon 12), jogging along stolidly for eons without changing. Others are flighty and unstable (carbon 14), and it is these more ephemeral varieties that are our concern here. An unstable form is called a radionuclide because it can spontaneously change or decay into the nuclide of another element, radiating energy in the process. For example, the unstable radionuclide carbon 14 can decay into the highly stable gas nitrogen 14, and in the process it emits energy as various forms of radiation, radiation we shall have to distinguish and think about carefully later.

It is this property of spontaneous radioactive decay that we use for an enormous number of highly beneficial purposes, ranging from archaeology to medicine. We cannot tell when an individual atom is going to decay, but we know with great precision the overall rate at which the quadrillions of atoms of carbon 14 in an old piece of wood or charcoal will decay to half their amount. The time taken to reach this "halflife" lets us work backwards and calculate when an ax handle, spear shaft or cooking fire was used hundreds, or even thousands of years ago. In medicine, radioactive cobalt 60 is a powerful source of radiation that can be carefully focused on cancerous tumors, while minute amounts of other radioactive nuclides can be monitored in the human body to disclose dangerous circulation problems. It is very important to realize that radioactivity is a natural phenomenon, a part of our ordinary physical world that includes the life-giving warmth from the sun, itself an enormous atomic furnace.

Uranium, and its common oxide used as atomic fuel, is also found in nature in two forms; the stable nuclide uranium 238 (about 99.3 percent), and an unstable radionuclide, uranium 235 (the remaining 0.7 percent). This small amount of uranium 235 is all that is left of what was around when the earth was first formed, but even this small amount is enough for human purposes. Carefully separated out, and used like a pinch of salt to flavor a soup, it can be used to enrich uranium oxide fuel pellets up to 2 percent, or about three times the level ordinarily found in nature today.

When an atom of uranium 235 decays spontaneously, it loses some of its energy in two ways. Part of it is lost as radiation, and part is lost as a release of some of the neutrons in the nucleus. These have a very high energy and move so quickly that it is unlikely they will bump into another atom of either uranium 235 or 238. Why particles moving very quickly are unlikely to bump into others is not intuitively obvious at first, so think of children running at random around a playground. Suppose you are standing on one side, trying to hit a spot on the opposite fence with a ball. Although the children are running around, most of the time they do not go between you and the spot you are trying to hit, and if you throw the ball very quickly you will probably get it to the target on the other side without a child getting in the way. On the other hand, if you could throw the ball very slowly, perhaps slowing it down to a snail's pace in some artificial way, it would almost certainly hit some scampering child during its molasses-like flight. The ball is our neutron, and the children are our atoms of uranium 235 and 238. We have to slow neutrons down in order to increase the chance of them hitting the uranium atoms in our fuel pellets.

When a loose neutron, from an atom of uranium 235 that has just spontaneously decayed, hits an atom of uranium 238 nothing immediately dramatic seems to happen. The neutron is simply absorbed, and the uranium 238 becomes another nuclide, uranium 239. Eventually this decays to plutonium 239, another radionuclide that can be used as a fuel in what are termed fast breeder reactors, reactors that literally can breed more fuel from common uranium 238 than they consume. Plutonium 239 is damnably dangerous stuff: it has been estimated that 2 kilograms (about 4.4 pounds) of plutonium 239 "properly distributed" (at this point language begins to break down under the obscenity that it is forced to carry), could kill every child, woman, and man on earth.

On the other hand, when a neutron on the loose hits an atom of uranium 235 it forces the atom to fission or split into two fragments, once again losing energy through radiation and the release of more high velocity neutrons. In the ordinary way, because they are moving so quickly, these may either be absorbed by the uranium 238 or more likely by some carefully constructed shielding material. But if they are somehow slowed down, or their velocity is moderated, then the chance of them hitting other atoms of uranium 235 goes up. Then the newly fissioning atoms release more, and now moderated neutrons in turn, which produce more and more and more ... until we have a chain reaction. Which is exactly what an atomic bomb is, for these reactions take place on time scales measured in billionths of seconds (nanoseconds), and so can release their energy with truly explosive force.

The trick, of course, is to find just that narrow range between total absorption of the neutrons and their uncontrolled release as a chain reaction. The task is to control atomic fission in such a way that we can release energy slowly in a usable and useful form. This is essentially an engineering problem, so it is back to Reactor 4 at Chernobyl. All four of the reactors at Chernobyl were modifications of a very simple design first constructed in the 1950s to produce plutonium 239 for atomic weapons. In a number of its basic design features it was not unlike its early counterparts in the United States (Hanford, Washington) and Britain (Windscale, Cumbria, now renamed Sellafield in an attempt to reduce public visibility after a catastrophic accident in 1957 rather similar to Chernobyl).

All these earlier reactors for atomic weapons used graphite as a moderator, but there was one crucially important difference in the designs. The reactors at Chernobyl used the graphite almost solely as a moderator to slow down the neutrons, supplemented by the enormous flow of pressurized water–steam mixture, because water also captures and slightly moderates the speed of neutrons. As long as the proportions of water and steam were flowing properly, carrying off the energy as heat, and slightly moderating the neutron flow, all was well. But any overheating, or even worse, pump failure, would increase the proportion of steam, and then the voids produced by the bubbles would capture fewer neutrons. These would then enter the graphite, be effectively moderated, produce more fission, more energy, more heat, and over certain, rather low ranges of operation lead to an uncontrolled chain reaction. The design had a *positive void coefficient*, or the property, an engineer might say, of positive feedback – one increase leads to another and this leads to another ... and so on, until the "system" tears itself apart. There is nothing terribly technical or unfamiliar about positive feedback, for we have all experienced family rows. Joyce says something that is interpreted as a little unkind by her mother, who says something a bit sharp back, that is taken by Joyce as quite unnecessary, so she replies in kind ... until a flaming row explodes and they storm off in silence. Nations do the same thing, only it is called "escalation," and the explosion at the end of all the positive feedback is called "war."

In contrast, all reactors used in the West, including the earliest, were deliberately designed to have *negative void coefficients* over all ranges of their operations. Many of them, including Three Mile Island (TMI) in Pennsylvania, use water both to carry away the heat and to moderate the reaction. In these light water reactors, any steam voids or bubbles in the cooling and moderating flow mean fewer neutrons moderated, which leads to less fissioning, less energy, and less heat, until the process shuts itself off. They are all examples of negative feedback that clamps things down. Unfortunately, this does not mean that an accident cannot happen. Remember the temperatures of the fuel rods are extremely high, and if something happens to reduce the water flow suddenly – a pipe ruptures, a pump breaks down – then the heat can melt the fuel cladding and pipes, come into instantaneous contact with the water, and so produce a flash steam explosion. Or worse: at those extreme temperatures, water molecules (H_2O) can split into their hydrogen and oxygen components. Hydrogen itself is highly explosive, and oxygen provides an atmosphere in which pure carbon (the graphite block) catches fire to burn at extremely high temperatures. These temperatures are so high that water sprayed on a huge mass of burning graphite never reaches it, and may only contribute more oxygen to the atmosphere to make the graphite burn even hotter. There is some evidence from eye witnesses and computer monitors at Chernobyl that a second explosion, 3 or 4 seconds after the main one, involved a very rapid buildup of hydrogen, caused by the graphite core igniting and sustaining itself in an oxygen-rich atmosphere.

But whether the void coefficients are positive or negative, almost all atomic reactors are potentially highly dangerous beasts to have by their tails, and they require the very highest standards of engineering design, highly trained and alert operators, extreme caution at all times, and a clear and established set of procedures to deal with any conceivable emergency. These might include sudden mechanical failures of all sorts, earthquakes, operator failures, computer failures, and even deliberate sabotage by terrorist attack. It takes an enormous amount of technical knowledge to control – that is genuinely and properly control – an atomic reactor in that twilight state between no reaction and sudden flash buildup to explosion. What controls are there?

People first: but people can fall asleep or be lulled by years of boredom into such a feeling of lethargic security that there might be little control in an emergency. In the United States, control operators have been dismissed for dereliction of duty, but the job still remains boring for their replacements. Secondly, there are machines, particularly computers, and these are being used increasingly to monitor and operate reactors. However, the computers must be large and fast, and programmed in such a way that they can react to any possible combination of circumstances. This means that engineers have thought through everything that can go wrong, including human beings going beserk, or perhaps deliberately ignoring or disobeying carefully laid out instructions and procedures.

This means machines now control people. And a damned good thing too, many scientists would say. Computers never get tired, or bored, or fall asleep at the job, and they can often react much faster in an emergency than human beings can. After all, and to make it quite immediate and personal, if you were in a post-operative ward, and had to have dozens of literally vital signals from your body monitored, which would you rather have, a tired, perhaps exhausted and stressed human nurse, or a tireless computer always ready to signal if something goes wrong? But we have to be careful with this analogy, because there is a difference here. Blood pressure, raised or lowered beyond certain threshold values, is immediately signalled ... to whom? To a human being, a nurse or doctor, who knows what to do. But in controlling atomic reactors, human decisions may not be fast enough, or may actually inject grievous error into an already complex situation, so human actions may have to be overridden by the machine. We are entering a very difficult area here, fraught with deeply ethical implications, precisely the sort of issues that make us humans and not machines. Juvenal once wrote "*quis custodiet ipsos Custodes*," who guards the guards? Today we may have to face the question "*quis custodiet ipsos Computes?*"

Computers also require a steady supply of electricity, and so do all the other controlling machines. We shall see how worry over this need for an emergency supply of electrical power actually led to the Chernobyl disaster, but we need one final piece of technical and engineering information first. The major control on the rate of atomic fission in a reactor at Chernobyl is exerted by 211 control rods which can be inserted into the reactor from the top and bottom. These are made from boron carbide (B_4C) covered with an aluminum sleeve, and boron is an exceptionally good element for absorbing neutrons, stopping them dead in their tracks so that they cannot go on to hit more fuel atoms. By very carefully adjusting how many control rods are in place, and how deeply they are inserted, the neutron flux can be adjusted to that delicate point where fissioning takes place to produce controlled energy for power rather than a runaway chain reaction. Some of the rods are under manual control of the operators, some are automatically controlled by the monitoring computers, while a third group are scram rods, used for emergency shutdown if any local overheating is detected in the graphite pile. By adjusting combinations of rods, including short rods from the bottom, the temperature and the "shape" of the reaction – the actual three-dimensional volume fissioning in the pile – can be delicately controlled.

Such control, of course, requires very careful monitoring of the water, gas, and structural temperatures, the rates of flow, and even the thickness of the graphite blocks that slightly enlarge or shrink the insertion holes with changes in temperature. Constant monitoring of all these things takes place at 6,234 points in the pile, and the information is fed directly to the computers, or appears as cartograms – map-like pictures – for the human operators. Obviously, no group of human beings could monitor, evaluate, and react precisely and quickly to such an enormous flow of information. Machines are necessary to control machines, including emergency backup systems in case of failure. And that includes the failure of the electricity supply, a total power blackout that requires an emergency supply to run the computers that lower the control rods that stop the fissioning that signal the emergency pumps that stop the meltdown that causes the explosion that blows off the top of the reactor at Chernobyl.

3 So what happened at Chernobyl?

One of the major worries of engineers who design and operate nuclear reactors is the possibility of a complete power failure, an electricity blackout that would immediately stop all the automatic monitoring and control devices, including the pumps that force the huge quantities of cooling and moderating water through the fissioning pile. Even in reactors with negative void coefficients a lack or reduction of cooling water quickly results in the fuel rods melting, with the almost certain danger of a flash steam explosion. Obviously some sort of backup system is needed, and *all* reactors have such systems. So did Reactor 4 at Chernobyl.

In North America and western Europe, most countries follow the example of the United States, where, by law, all atomic reactors must have massive battery systems that can cut in instantaneously in the case of power failure, and especially designed diesel generators that can go from a cold start to full power in 10 seconds. The auxiliary diesel generators used at Chernobyl required 45 seconds to come to full power, and in that critical interval some other source of electricity was needed. The solution of the Soviet engineers was ingenious. Electricity was generated at Chernobyl by large and rapidly spinning dynamos, and these would not stop immediately even if the steam was suddenly shut off. It would take a minute or two for them to "spin down," and while they were losing momentum and slowing down there was no reason they could not go on turning the generators to produce a small amount of electricity. The question was whether this reserve of "spin power" from an unpowered, but still turning generator could fill the critical gap before the diesels took over.

It was an important test, although one wonders how anyone could have brought an atomic reactor into that delicate state of controlled fission *before* testing such a crucial safety feature. It would have been perfectly possible to test the spin of similar generators on conventional, coal-fired plants to see if they could supply enough electrical power to fill the gap. Nevertheless, the engineers chose to conduct the test while the reactor was in operation. It had become the normal, and therefore unthinking way of doing things, because these sorts of tests had been conducted many times before on other reactors at Chernobyl, and on similar power plants using the same technology around the country.

It was essentially an electrical test conducted by electrical engineers, and no one seems to have really connected it with any problem of reactor operation. The people who carried out the test did so without the approval of those in charge of safety procedures, but the test had become so routine that approval was only a formality anyway. The trouble with science and technology today is that the sheer volume of knowledge is so enormous that no one can possibly grasp more than a small part of it. The result is ever-higher degrees of specialization, with more and more people forced by the circumstances of our scientific and technological world to live in smaller and smaller boxes increasingly disconnected from the rest. Electrical engineers live in one specialized box, and atomic engineers live in another, and rarely shall the twain meet because they have only very general concepts and mathematical languages to connect them. But mathematical languages do not care what meaning is given to them, and general concepts are often not good enough in a world of highly specialized ideas. So we see the "disconnection" at Chernobyl as one poignant example of a much larger problem of our world. And there is no escape.

It is not necessary to go into every detail of the sequence of events leading to the catastrophe, a sequence meticulously reconstructed by the Soviets and reported with quite extraordinary openness on a minute by minute, and even second by second, basis to the United Nations' International Atomic Energy Agency at Vienna. What has become clear is that one safety regulation after another was overridden by the people conducting the test, until there was no chance of reversing the events of the last few seconds. We shall have to condense a long, detailed and technical story leading to a nightmare, a nightmare involving 1,680 fuel rods, 211 control rods, 6,234 information flows, and a group of people almost oblivious to the dangers involved. What happened at Chernobyl was this.

A previous test had shown that while the actual spin power of the generators was probably sufficient to fill the gap, the voltage they produced was too irregular as the turbines lost their momentum. A new voltage regulating system had been put in, and it was this that was really the focus of the test run. By very slowly inserting the control rods, the power was gradually reduced during the previous day. A slow reduction was necessary to avoid the buildup of xenon gas in the core, a gas that interferes with the moderating process and makes control more difficult. When half power was reached in the early afternoon, one of the generators was shut down, and the emergency cooling system for the core was disconnected to prevent it from cutting in automatically during the test – when everything would be under control anyway.

At this point the test was interrupted for about 9 hours because the electricity was needed to supply an unexpected demand. When the test was resumed later that night power was reduced still further, and then a switch was made from a computer control system that was very sensitive to local changes of temperature and pressure to a more general, or global system that tended to average these local effects away. As a result, both reactor and steam power dropped rapidly into the very dangerous zone of operation where the positive void coefficient ruled. To correct this situation, control rods were removed by hand to increase the reactor power, but in a low power range the more control rods that are withdrawn the more positive the void coefficient becomes, and the more sensitive the reactor is to small local fluctuations. And these were no longer being monitored directly anyway, but being smoothed and averaged out to more general values.

This was not a happy state of affairs, but by fiddling with a control rod here and there, and adjusting the flow of water through the pile, the operators managed to hit on a low, but stable power output. It was also a level forbidden by safety regulations, and it resembled the stability of someone teetering on a balance beam that is narrowing down and down to a knife edge. At low power levels the compensating relations between the steam voids, the water pressure and flow, and the temperature and the neutron flux are very delicate, the sort an engineer would call "non-linear." This means that they do not rise and fall in relation to each other in simple straightforward ways, and it is not immediately and intuitively obvious what even a small system will do when it is held together by these sorts of non-linear connections. It is not too much of an exaggeration to say that the last 20 minutes at Chernobyl were like a modern Promethean battle to steal the fire from the gods on Mount Olympus.

As water pressure was increased to reduce the steam bubbles or voids, it also lowered the temperature causing more voids to collapse. This meant fewer neutrons were captured and moderated and less power produced. So now the automatic control rods started pulling out to increase the neutron flux, and some of the manual rods were also withdrawn to maintain a proper power balance. At this point the operator switched off the automatic pressure controls because these seemed to be causing fluctuations. Just as the human operators were trying to stabilize things one way, the machines were trying another. And since the machines refused to play according to the new rules, in a forbidden area of operation for which they had not been programmed, they were thrown out of the game.

But now the temperature rose, and to control this more water was forced through to carry the excess heat away. This caused the pressure to rise in the steam–water mixture, so the water flow was cut back. With less water flow, more steam voids appeared, more neutrons were moderated, triggering the reinsertion of the control rods to soak up the excess neutron flux. Finally nature seemed to be under control, because a rather fragile stability had been achieved, and at last the test started. The emergency trip signal to the second generator on the other side of the reactor was switched off, so that if the test had to be repeated there was another unit that could spin down to try out the new system. Unfortunately the water flow was decreasing again, because some of the cooling pumps were running slower with the spin down of the generator under test. Steam began to build up, voids appeared, and more neutrons were moderated by the graphite.

The last few seconds ticked away, and as the power level started to surge the final "panic button" was pressed to bring about a total shutdown. It was too late. Too many manual rods had been withdrawn, and the automatic scram rods could not be inserted fast enough. In that dark region of the positive void coefficient the dreaded uncontrolled chain reaction started. Within 3 or 4 seconds the reactor power exploded from about 5 percent to 100 times its normal level, shattering the fuel rods that instantaneously turned the water into steam. The flash pressure ruptured the fuel channels in the graphite and lifted the upper plate of the reactor. A thousand tons of steel and concrete flipped like a penny. A second explosion occurred a few seconds after the first. No one to this day is quite sure why. It might have been a second power "excursion," the sober euphemism scientists use for all hell breaking loose, or it might have been a result of hydrogen buildup as the water split into its constituent hydrogen–oxygen parts. Whatever the reason, it completed the job by shattering the pile and its concrete housing, throwing burning graphite and a score of different radionuclides over the surrounding area and high into the atmosphere.

We shall take a very careful look at the radioactive components of the nuclear cloud that spewed from shattered Reactor 4 during the nine days following the accident. To do this properly we shall have to make another short scientific excursion to see how radioactivity and its radiation are measured, but these aspects of the physical world can be set aside for the moment. They are totally overshadowed by a human drama of such stirring courage that the men and women who took part, and who gave their lives, will be forever honored. If the name Chernobyl stands for human folly and Promethean arrogance, it also stands for courage of the highest order. And cowardice too.

4 Courage and cowardice

Now began days that were truly heroic, a word in Soviet rhetoric to which we have become almost inured, honoring its true meaning at a Stalingrad, but dismissing it as hyperbole and political puff when applied to production targets. But let no one doubt the courage and bravery of those who fought the fires in those immediate days after the explosion, fires that pushed more and more radionuclides into the intense convection plume, increasing the radioactive radiation to lethal levels in the local areas. Some were ignorant of the exact dangers involved, but kept going until they dropped. Others knew only too well what was at stake, and chose to give their lives that others might live. A few had other things to do at that moment, things that took them from the immediate scene. Some, who had lived their official lives in a bureaucratic hierarchy numbing to individual initiative and responsibility, failed to take decisions that could have saved the lives of others. The courage outweighs the cowardice many fold, and we must honor the first, pity the second, and try to understand both.

When the reactor exploded, the debris immediately buried and killed one of the senior operators in the reactor hall, where his body still lies today. The radiation and heat from the stricken pile was so intense that no one was ever able to get near him again. A second operator rushed into the hall to see what had happened, and received such an intense dose of radiation from the unshielded core and the radioactive debris that he died a few hours later, his final agony comforted by the sheltering arms of a nurse at the station. She was his wife. No formal fire warning was needed. The sound of the explosion brought the 15 men in Reactor 4's fire fighting unit immediately to the scene, but more than 30 fires had already been started by the white hot and radioactive pieces of graphite that had been blown from the core, and the men were simply overwhelmed by the task they faced. When the larger unit from the town of Chernobyl, 16 kilometers (10 miles) away arrived, the flames had almost reached the roof of the ten-story hall housing the generators. The fire chief immediately sent out a Stage Three alarm, the highest emergency level, and eventually more than 300 men and women were brought to the reactor, some from as far away as Kiev, 80 kilometers (50 miles) to the south.

By this time everyone knew what dangers were involved. By four o'clock in the morning some of the original fire fighters were weak and vomiting, the sure signs of intense radiation sickness, but no one turned back. Some fought the fire from the roof 30 meters (100 feet) up, trying to direct their hoses down onto the flames to prevent them from spreading to the adjacent Reactor 3, and to stop the collapse of the roof on which they were standing. This was now a quagmire of thick melted bitumen and tar, sticking to the boots of the firemen and making their efforts even more difficult. The intense fires of the smaller graphite pieces were eventually put out by high pressure water hoses and foam blankets, but nothing could extinguish the fire in the graphite core. From the first moments the operators had turned on emergency pumps in the reactor room, pushing tons of water through until the flood started to wash towards the other reactors, carrying radioactive debris with it. But as soon as the water got near the graphite core it was immediately turned to steam, and the convection plume was so intense that no foams could blanket the burning pile. As soon as the flood started to endanger the other reactors the pumps were switched off and the pile allowed to burn. In those first few hours there was nothing else to do.

Doctors and nurses were also called, and gave of their skills totally unselfishly and with great courage. One doctor on night duty at the nearby Pripyat clinic made trip after trip to pull sick and exhausted firemen from the destruction, until he realized that he had the "metal taste" in his own mouth, an almost sure symptom of intense radiation sickness. He too died from overexposure shortly afterwards. Some of the firemen were so intensely exposed that their bodies and clothing endangered those who tried to help them. More than 300 men and women were hospitalized, and 31 died within a few hours, days or weeks despite highly skilled and compassionate efforts to save them. These included bone marrow transplant operations by a visiting American specialist, and advice from his colleagues from both the United States and Israel, but in most cases the radiation damage was too severe. Few of the 13 people receiving the transplants survived, either because the transplants did not take, or because their other internal injuries were so severe that they had little chance. Medical visitors who witnessed the efforts of Soviet doctors and nurses to bring people back to health have been unstinting in their praise and admiration. Even after sending more than 200 burn and radiation victims to Moscow hospitals, and others to Kiev, there were simply not enough supersterile burn wards to house everyone. Soviet doctors took over ordinary wards, and with jerry rigged ultraviolet lamps created the necessary sterile conditions for the deep burns to heal.

A Stage Three fire alarm at an atomic reactor brought quick attention

from higher authorities. By four o'clock that morning a disaster headquarters had been set up by the Ukraine's deputy minister of internal
affairs, a major general, and by six o'clock road blocks had been set up by
the militia to restrict all unnecessary traffic, clearing the roads for fire
fighting equipment and ambulances. Soldiers and police also carried
radiation counters to monitor both people and vehicles. People in the
local area were told to remain indoors if possible, and to keep their
windows closed. Iodine pills were distributed to all children in order to
saturate their thyroid glands with ordinary iodine, and so prevent them
taking up the radionuclide iodine 131. One woman had not known about
the accident, and in her innocence walked across the fields in the early
morning sunshine to her work in the kitchens. She quickly felt severe
radiation burns where the long grass had brushed radioactive particles
onto her legs.

Moscow had also been informed, and only 2 hours after the explosion a
team of radiation experts was ready. They arrived at noon that day and
began to monitor the radiation levels at Pripyat and nearby villages. At
that time the initial radiation levels in the town were not that high,
certainly not high enough to order evacuation. In the first hours, the
winds were carrying the fallout in a different direction, one that lay over
potential evacuation routes. Radiation was catastrophic in the building,
and very high in the immediate area where heavier particles had fallen, but
most of the debris and radionuclides from the pile had been carried by the
initial explosion and the intense heat of the convection plume high into
the sky. The pattern of radioactive fallout was very complex and spotty,
depending literally on which way the wind blew. We shall see just how
far it blew later.

The question of evacuating the entire area around the plant must have
arisen soon after the explosion. During those first critical hours members
of Komsomol, the young communist organization, had come forward to
help, and by eight o'clock that morning they were making door-to-door
visits to give the potassium iodide tablets to children and to advise people
to stay indoors for the time being. But in a rigid bureaucratic system, in
which requests go up and directives come down deeply incised official
channels, no one was prepared to take the responsibility for such a
large-scale decision as evacuation. That all changed with the arrival that
evening of a deputy chairman of the Council of Ministers, a man known
for his decisiveness and problem solving ability. He immediately ordered
the evacuation of everyone in the surrounding area, including 45,000
people at nearby Pripyat, and so cleared the area to concentrate on the
basic problem of extinguishing the graphite fire. We shall follow the

evacuation, a major feat of organization and logistical planning, a little later.

The fire in the graphite core was so intense that it posed problems only faced once before in human history, when a similar fire in the Windscale (Sellafield) graphite reactor took hold in 1957. It took three days to put out the Windscale fire, which spewed large quantities (100–1,000 times that discharged by Three Mile Island) of radionuclides into the atmosphere, especially iodine 131. The British people were not, of course, told until three days later. This was after the radioactive cloud had been monitored over Holland (leading to a vigorous protest by the Dutch government), after the fire had been extinguished, and after the radioactive iodine had been allowed to enter the food chain from grass to cows to milk to children. All information was thoroughly suppressed during the first three critical days (it was, so ran the argument, a purely government and Whitehall matter, and one of the people's business) and also for 30 years afterwards under a rule invoked by the then Prime Minister, Harold Macmillan, that allowed these "sensitive" facts to be hidden from the public. We shall see a number of identical and parallel aspects in the case of Chernobyl, except that the Soviet government took much more rapid action in its own country, and once the facts were in it opened the entire incident to the view of international atomic experts so that valuable lessons could be learned. Most regrettably, no lessons were immediately available from the British experience, although a number of atomic engineers had more than an inkling of the dangers and difficulties involved.

Spraying the graphite fire in the reactor was useless, and perhaps even made things worse, so an alternative three-pronged attack was tried, organized by a deputy director of the Kurchatov Institute of Atomic Energy in Moscow. He directed the operation over the following days and weeks, forbidding his appalled subordinates to tell him what radiation doses had been monitored on his personal and blackened film badges. Somehow oxygen had to be excluded, and the intense radioactivity absorbed. Helicopter pilots began dropping 800 tons of dolomite to produce large quantities of carbon dioxide to blanket the flames, and 40 tons of boron carbide to absorb neutron activity. They also dropped 1,800 tons of clay and sand to help exclude oxygen and to filter the radionuclides passing continually into the atmosphere in the high convection plume. Finally 2,400 tons of lead were dropped to absorb heat upon melting, and to make a liquid layer that might seal the core when it solidified again. All these materials had to be dropped with pinpoint accuracy on the exposed and burning core, and this could only be done by hovering low and directly over it. Some of the helicopter pilots refused to disclose the radiation readings to which they had been exposed, fearing that they would be grounded and their efforts jeopardized. An airforce general had to plead with them, saying that fresh crews had come forward and the work would go on.

Dumping more than 5,000 tons of material on the core raised the possibility of deforming and breaking the floor of the reactor, and there was also the additional fear that the burning graphite might cut its way through the thick reinforced concrete of the reactor platform. Either eventuality would allow huge quantities of radionuclides to enter and contaminate the ground water and drinking supplies over the entire drainage area. Miners from the Donbas coal fields volunteered to take on the dangerous and difficult task of digging beneath the reactor by constructing reinforcements to prevent a collapse. But now yet another problem arose. In the first five days after the initial explosion the radioactive discharge gradually declined due to the efforts of the helicopter pilots. But the very solution to the problem now backfired. By blanketing the pile in dolomite, sand, clay, and lead the heat began to build up again, and by the sixth day (May 2) the radionuclide discharges soared once again to alarming levels. As we shall see, this second peak of the discharge was also monitored around the world. It was like the fable of the Sorcerer's Apprentice: solve the fire fighting by dumping and excluding oxygen, and you either push the reactor into the ground, or you block the avenue for heat to escape. Finally, on May 5, as the discharges were building up to levels approaching those of the first day, the task force managed to get a pipeline carrying liquid nitrogen under the reactor room, and this icy liquid finally did the trick, absorbing the intense heat, and blanketing the entire reactor with an envelope of inert gas.

For ten days it had been a truly dramatic fight, calling for the most courageous and generous efforts of many fire fighters, doctors, nurses, miners, pilots, and administrators. But in its ground it was a human story, and so contained within it the possibility of cowardice and the "I'm-in-the-boat-Jack ... shove-off" syndrome that marks the other human response to fear. A number of officials in charge of plant operations were summarily fired for failing to stay on the job, or because they had packed up their families and left without warning others. One young couple in Pripyat fled their home, leaving behind their old invalid father. Only his single light in a blackened apartment building told police that someone was still there. Under the more open conditions of *glasnost*, the sad, but all-too-human acts are told in some of the most moving lines of the remarkable play *Sarcophagus*. The play was written by a science correspondent of *Pravda*, sent by his editor to report during the first few weeks after the accident. The scale of the disaster, the courage and cowardice of those who were involved, and his conversations with the men dying of radiation sickness overwhelmed him. He felt newspaper reports could never convey the human drama, so he sat down and wrote the play in a few weeks. It was published two months later, and was soon playing to packed theatres in Leningrad, Stockholm, and London. As the drama unfolds, an investigator interviews one of the directors of the plant in a special ward for radiation victims:

Investigator	I have only a few questions ... You were not at the power station at the time, were you?
Director	I wasn't able to be, but I was at the very beginning.
Investigator	Did you realize at once what had happened?
Director	More or less. In general terms.
Investigator	And you left the station?
Director	I, er, temporarily absented myself. You see ...
Investigator	I know. Your grandchildren were alone at home.
Director	I saw that work was in hand to extinguish the reactor. My son's mother-in-law lives in a village nearby, eight kilometers away. I thought I'd just dash over to the village, leave my grandsons there and come straight back.
Investigator	But why didn't you alert the whole town? Then they could all have dashed out into the country, even if only, say, five kilometers up-wind. They could have gone that far on foot. It only needed an announcement on the local radio to notify everybody. There was no need for them to wait those twenty-four hours until the official evacuation order was given.
Director	It's not as simple as that.
Investigator	But to put your grandsons into your car and drive away – that was simpler, was it? After all, you knew better than anyone else what had happened. Yet children were still playing football in town *this morning*. And freshly picked cucumbers were being brought in and sold on the streets ...
Director	I couldn't get back. You know why. They must have told you.
Investigator	Yes – a silly accident. Your car skidded off the road and got stuck on the verge for a quarter of an hour. Fortunately, your grandsons didn't get out of the car. Yes, I know about that. And on the way back you were stopped and detained for a medical check.
Director	I had driven right through the "dirtiest" area of the fallout.

Those who know about the dangers of radiation, yet assure others that nothing can possibly go wrong, are often the first to take actions to save only themselves when something does go wrong, ignoring everyone else around them. These sorts of behavior are just part of the human condition, the dark underside to shining courage, and we shall come across rather similar contradictions in other countries.

Extinguishing the graphite core was only the beginning of the end, an end that may come only tens of thousands of years from now. What do you do with a reactor that has gone wrong? How do you clean things up in the presence of such radioactivity? There is only one thing to do with the reactor and that is seal it off, isolate it, cover it up in such a way that the intense radiation can never come into contact with any living system again. Hence the play's title *Sarcophagus*, a tomb befitting such a device. Bessmertny, a character in the play who has survived a dose of radiation thought to be lethal, says:

> Just imagine: none of us will be here, not even our great-great-great-grandchildren. All our cities will have gone ... Even the pyramids of Egypt will be just a handful of dust, yet the sarcophagus around this reactor of yours will still be standing. The pyramids of the Pharaohs have been there for a mere five thousand years. But to contain the radiation your nuclear pyramid must remain for at least a hundred thousand years ... That's some monument to leave our descendants, isn't it? ... they'll see what *sort* of Raphaels, Michelangelos and Leonardos lived in the twentieth century.

But those hundred thousand years started in the days and weeks after the incident. What did people do?

5 Exodus from Wormwood

Although the order to evacuate the immediate area was delayed for 24 hours, the entire operation was organized very quickly once the order had been given. Those in charge faced enormous logistical problems that had to be overcome rapidly, because radiation levels were now beginning to rise with the continual flow of radionuclides pouring out of the plume. The people of Pripyat and villages within a 10 kilometer (6 mile) zone around the reactor were evacuated first. They had been told to stay indoors by the Komsomol volunteers, but some out of curiosity evaded the roadblocks and exposed themselves to severe doses of radiation. A second round of door-to-door visits told everyone to be ready by the early afternoon, and in the 12 hours available 1,100 buses were brought from as far away as Kiev and Odessa. On a Saturday night and early Sunday morning bus drivers were hard to find, but rumors were starting to spread and many came forward sensing that something terrible had happened. Lists were prepared of the people to be evacuated, and buses with sufficient capacity were assigned to sectors of the town. Many collecting points were better than a few in order to minimize the time people had to be out of doors in dry and dusty conditions. The dust now held large radionuclide particles that had settled out of the plume first, and these could do great damage to human lung tissue. Evacuation routes had to be established, something that was no easy matter because the fallout had been spotty and uneven, which meant that "safe channels" through the radioactivity had to be found. A major route of evacuation led north from the area, a zone particularly heavily contaminated by the heavier particles. Parts of the roadside verges were covered with polymer film to keep the dust down, but bus drivers who made repeated trips were contaminated more than others. Radiation monitoring and medical stations had to be prepared to check all the evacuees, and eventually 13,000 doctors and nurses were involved in the operation. Shelter and food also had to be made available to house the initial influx of 45,000 people within the inner zone of radioactivity, and this was only the first phase of a much larger evacuation plan.

By two o'clock that Sunday afternoon the first evacuations took place, a 12 mile convoy of buses carrying the people of Pripyat and nearby villages north to permanent resettlement in northern Byelorussia. Three hours later the town was deserted. Well, almost deserted. In the surrounding rural villages many were particularly reluctant to leave. After all, who was going to look after the animals? Some simply refused to leave them behind, and eventually trucks were found to evacuate the larger animals as well. Only then did the owners consent to leave, following their cows and pigs to the decontamination points where they were washed down. Even in Pripyat not everyone was prepared to leave their familiar surroundings and the precious personal belongings that had been gathered together over a lifetime. Two elderly ladies hid indoors from all the patrols and lived on water and canned food for 34 days before they were finally discovered. Other elderly people evaded all the cordons and patrols, and sneaked back to recover their precious possessions or to feed their pets. "God knows how they did it," said the major general in charge of the militia, "But the old ladies would creep back to their yards, and when our patrols found them they would burst out crying, stubbornly asking who would look after their geese and chickens." Today the town of Pripyat, the surrounding villages, and all the farms lie abandoned, and all human activity has been banned. Animals are coming back, and foxes are multiplying rapidly in the human-free area. What the ultimate effects on animals will be no one knows.

Yet even as these massive evacuation plans were being carried out most people in the Soviet Union still had no inkling of the catastrophe. Party officials in Moscow were told immediately that "there had been a fire at Chernobyl," but there was no sign of any public announcement. Rumors spread rapidly in Kiev and Chernobyl, and in the smaller towns supplying buses and drivers, but most had little idea of what had really happened. The day after the accident the people in the town of Chernobyl, 15 kilometers (9 miles), away were going about their ordinary tasks, fixing things up in the sunshine of a pleasant spring weekend. One Ukrainian writer was painting his small boat, getting it ready for fishing; others were digging and raking, getting their gardens ready for the first sowing. Despite the new and much publicized policy of *glasnost* the old bureaucratic reaction to cover things up still ruled.

Such reactions are not confined to the Soviet bureaucracy; it is the natural reaction of *any* bureaucracy to smother "unfortunate news." The suppression of information is the arrogant and endemic curse of all modern bureaucracies, a curse that is constitutive of what they are. But in the same way that the graphite fire could not be smothered, so its consequences could not be blanketed and suppressed for long. That soaring plume was no respecter of international boundaries, and only 30 hours after the initial explosion the secret was out. As we shall see,

Finland, Sweden, and Poland were picking up unprecedented amounts of radionuclides in the atmosphere, and their "fingerprint spectrum" identified a reactor accident rather than a bomb test above ground. By Sunday evening Sweden's ambassador was making strong representations to Moscow, and on the nine o'clock news that morning from Moscow, 56 hours after the accident, a terse three-sentence statement about a fire at Chernobyl was read out.

There is some reasonable evidence that even Moscow did not fully appreciate the extent and seriousness of the damage until the full team of top administrators and experts from the scientific institutes arrived on the scene. The head of the Kurasov Research Institute, who supervised much of the cleanup and prepared the official report at Vienna, said frankly "I won't hide the fact that I had not supposed the size of the accident was as great as it actually was. It was only on driving to Pripyat and seeing the glow that I began to guess the nature of what had happened. To assess what was going on from Moscow was impossible." Even so, for another 32 hours the public's "need to know" was dismissed out of hand.

Within the next six days another 90,000 people were evacuated from a 30 kilometer (18 mile) zone around the reactor, and in the weeks that followed 64,000 children in southern Byelorussia in the direct path of the plume, and 25,000 more from Kiev, were evacuated to summer camps. Evacuation plans depended on which way the wind was blowing the convection plume at the time, a plume that continued to carry radionuclides high into the sky. Whichever way it blew, the heaviest and most dangerous particles settled out first, creating a spotty patchwork quilt of radioactivity that had to be crossed like a child playing hopscotch on a pavement. Fortunately in those early days there was no rain to scavenge the particles from the plume, because all the rain-bearing clouds were seeded from airplanes with silver iodide to make them disperse or give up their moisture before they could get over the Chernobyl area.

At Kiev, 140 kilometers (80 miles) to the south, there was no significant radioactivity during the first week, and information was so sparse that few people worried. The national holiday of May 1 came and went with people enjoying parades and spring sunshine, although some participants from eastern Europe found it difficult to make the starting line of a big cycle race and cancelled out. Only on May 5, when a wind shift carried a second surge of activity from the now blanketed and damped down pile, did Kiev receive any appreciable fallout. The minister of health televised a warning that people should stay indoors, and street sales of all foodstuffs were banned. People were advised to wash their hair, clothes and themselves frequently, because the greatest enemy was the dust. Even six weeks later the streets were washed down three times a day to keep the dust down, and each time the wind blew fresh dust from the north the radioactivity levels rose. At the doors of shops, houses, and hotels wet cloths were available for people to wipe their shoes. Some particles clung to the shoes of visitors from Holland, and when they went home Dutch radiologists lifted the specks of various radionuclides with sticky tape and made a careful analysis of their size and radioactivity.

The routines of daily life in Kiev and other smaller towns changed quite markedly. Kiev became a city without children for many months, and a city without many young mothers who had taken their babies away. By May 7, long lines had formed at the railway stations and airports, and extra planes and trains were scheduled. Some doctors advised their pregnant patients to have abortions and many did so, although there was no general directive or recommendation. Soccer and volleyball were strongly discouraged because of the dust kicked up and inhaled in such vigorous games, and for a while swimming was banned in the Dnepr River. Although it was denied for many months, the level of radioactivity in the Dnepr was so high that Kiev's main water supply was switched to the Desna River and artesian wells. All vegetables sold by local farmers in the famous Bessarabskaya Market or from street stalls had to be checked for radioactivity, and the market women gathered at four in the morning to get their slips of paper stamped guaranteeing safe produce. "No Radiation, No Radiation" was added to the old and familiar market cries of "Apples . . . Strawberries . . . Cherries."

Much cherished spring herbs and the fresh shoots of sorrel and chives were among the first vegetables to be banned because the contamination was so high. Perhaps it was the absence of these traditional and much anticipated signs of spring that led the country folk to recall another wild herb in a passage from The Revelation of St John the Divine, the book of the Apocalypse that has always formed a part of the Bible for the Ukrainian Orthodox Church. "Do you remember" they said , "in chapter 8, verses 10 and 11, where the angels are sounding their trumpets of doom?"

> When the third angel blew his trumpet a great star flaming like a torch descended from the sky, falling upon the third part of the rivers and upon the sources of the water. The star is called Wormwood. The third part of the waters turned to wormwood, and great numbers of men died from drinking the waters because they had been poisoned.

Wormwood is a bitter herb, used traditionally by country folk as a spring tonic. In Ukrainian its name is . . . *chernobyl.*

6 Where do you put it when it won't go away?

Even as the 135,000 people and thousands of animals were evacuated during that first week, plans for decontaminating the site and the surrounding area were drawn up. Despite severe contamination problems at the Soviet Union's atomic plants at Kyshtym in the 1950s, there was little guidance for those responsible for the cleanup at Chernobyl. Today the efforts they made are doubly valuable because they are the only real experience we have of dealing with such a catastrophe. The trouble with radioactive contamination is that it cannot be destroyed except by letting things take their course through natural decay. For the radionuclide iodine 131, which has a halflife of about 8 days, this means that in a couple of months the radiation is only about 1/200th of what it was – still nothing to dismiss out of hand if enough was around in the first place. But strontium 90 and caesium 137 have halflives of 28 and 30 *years*, while the halflife of plutonium 239 is 24,000 years. Unlike ordinary materials, which can be destroyed or made safe by chemical reactions, or perhaps by firing at high incinerator temperatures, the radionuclides are indestructible except to the physical laws of natural radioactive decay.

So how do you approach this difficult problem of getting rid of things that will not go away? There are only two ways of disconnecting them from living systems, whether these are algae or plants or animals or human beings. One is to dilute them, to make their presence in air or water so small that they can never be concentrated again to intensities damaging to life. As we shall see, this may not be so easy given the ability of certain life forms to filter large quantities of water and air, and in the process accumulate very dilute amounts of radionuclides back into damaging quantities. The second way is to trap these materials and somehow store them out of harm's way, but as Bessmertny's comment at the end of the play *Sarcophagus* reflected, because of plutonium 239's halflife, any structure storing it would have to stand five times as long as the pyramids.

At the highly contaminated site a dozen important steps had to be taken simultaneously, so there is no point in going down a checklist saying "First," "Second," "Third," and so on. The medical, ecological, and economic effects were all tightly intertwined, and it was a matter of multiple solutions on many fronts. The medical problems required an immediate cleanup and decontamination of the surrounding area once the pile had been exhausted and cooled with liquid nitrogen. This was a viciously difficult and dangerous task because the radiation levels were still lethally high. Simply to inspect the damage and to put equipment in place required approaching the damaged core and building wearing heavy protective clothing and special breathing masks and filters, but even so exposure times to radiation had to be carefully calculated, in some cases down to a maximum of 10–12 seconds. Even in that short period the maximum permissible lifetime dose was acquired, and people so exposed were taken off the job. One of the most severe prices the Soviet Union has had to pay as a result of the accident is that it has "used up" so many skilled people in its atomic power program. Many have now received the maximum lifetime dose permitted and can no longer be employed in their former, often highly skilled positions. A little later we shall have to take a careful look at how radiation is measured, a relatively uncontroversial question, and what various doses mean for human beings, a highly controversial question.

A lot of debris had to be cleared away using bulldozers and other heavy equipment, and despite lead shielding the manual operators were only allowed relatively short exposure times before they too were taken off. Remotely controlled equipment failed frequently in the early days and weeks because the intense radiation interfered with the electronic circuitry of the controls. Any electronic apparatus that could receive a radio instruction was also exposed to radiation levels that could upset the minute electrical currents characteristic of modern transistorized circuits. The stalled robots had to be approached by manually controlled machines and hauled away for repair. Over those summer and fall months Reactor 4 was slowly entombed in layers of shielding material and reinforced concrete over 1 meter (39 inches) thick, with monitoring devices throughout the huge structure to give immediate warning if anything should start to go wrong. The sarcophagus of Chernobyl is our monument, the pyramid of our technical age, a symbol of our achievements to the thousands of generations to come. Unfortunately, even the concrete shielding now in place is thought to be good only for 40–50 years, so the final solution still has to be faced. At the moment no one knows what to do.

At the same time that clearing up and entombment was taking place, other measures were also started. Extensive use was made of sprays to form a thin polymer film trapping the particles and suppressing the dangerous dust. In the immediate area 13,000 square meters (153,000 square yards) were laid down, about the area of 25 football fields, and more than 1,000 people slowly worked their way out from the most dangerous areas to locate other particularly bad "hot spots." These were also sprayed with what was described as "liquid glass," a clear polymer coating, at the rate of about 40 football fields a day – anything to fix the particles in place and prevent them from being carried by water and wind to contaminate other places, including human lung tissue. Washing was also tried, first on the walls, roofs, and equipment in the local area, especially Reactors 1, 2, and 3, and eventually on "hot" houses and barns up to 30 kilometers away. During the first few hours after the accident the ventilation systems had been left on, with the result that radioactive particles also contaminated the walls and surfaces of the three other reactor buildings. The reactors themselves had been shut down safely, but the economic effect on the Ukraine was severe, and decontamination had to be carried out quickly to bring them back into production. Even a year later they were staffed by people on two-week shifts, operators brought in from other plants around the country, partly to reduce exposure levels, partly to sensitize all nuclear power plant operators to the potentially dangerous possibilities.

The problem with trying to wash radioactivity away with water or solvents is that it produces another of those "damned if you do, damned if you don't" situations. Whatever liquids are used to remove the radionuclide dust and deposits they simply wash them into the soil or drainage system. There was the great fear that the radioactive particles would trickle through the soil and enter the ground water, and the same problem arose when water was sprayed to suppress dust in the dry conditions. The water kept the dust down but soil contamination went up. Once again this is the agonizing problem: you cannot get rid of the stuff, but only displace it from one place to another. So soil contamination also became a very serious matter, and over large areas the first 10 centimeters (4 inches) were scraped up and put in sealed containers. Full of highly contaminated soil, these then had to be disposed of. The question was where? Eventually the drums were placed in a waste repository at the site of Reactor 5, then just starting construction, but now indefinitely postponed.

One thing ecologists know is that "everything is connected to everything else." It is difficult to touch a filament of the delicate ecological web without feeling a tremble of effects throughout the system. Across wide areas of the Ukraine the fallout pattern produced grave problems for plants and animals – and therefore for people. Considerable areas were taken out of agricultural production, including a zone with a radius of 30 kilometers that is now a national park. All these areas are now being carefully monitored to learn as much as we can from this "experiment." Because dilution is seldom possible, and trapping and storing hundreds of square kilometers of soil quite infeasible, there is not much one can do to lower the intensity of the radioactivity. Ploughing the topsoil under may actually be worse than letting the land lie fallow. Not only does ploughing create large quantities of dust that can be inhaled, but the ploughshares may simply turn the top layers over, pushing the radionuclides into that zone from which the roots of crops draw most of their moisture and nutrients. The radioactivity buried in the spring ploughing rises systemically through the grains, vegetables, root and fodder crops to be harvested in the fall. It is like a deadly child's game of "Peekaboo." Thought you'd got rid of me? Here I am again!

Such a "game" is played with a vengeance in the woods and forests receiving the fallout, first in the crowns and leaves of the trees, later in the leaf litter that falls to the ground to decay into soil, releasing nutrients for further and constantly recycling growth. But while leaves decay in a season, radionuclides take their own halflives. In the immediate area around Chernobyl all the trees were severely damaged by radiation, and in a 3,000 square kilometer (1,200 square mile) area the trees were brown from the radioactivity. How one decontaminates such a huge area is anyone's guess. Burning the forest was suggested at one point, but this would only carry some of the particles still farther in the smoke, and the radioactive ashes would remain to be leached by rainfall into the soil and water table. Severe secondary contamination remains an ongoing problem, as radioactive dust blows back into Chernobyl to contaminate areas considered reasonably clean. It will be decades before the 800-year-old town becomes alive again with people calling it "home."

One visitor to Chernobyl, three years after the accident, provided a searing account of her experiences:

> Viktor is a haggard young engineer who was one of two people with primary responsibility for the containment of Reactor 4 after the explosion in 1986. In 60 seconds on the radioactive roof he was exposed to so [much radiation] that he cannot safely be exposed to any [more] until 1991. His skin turned black and came off his body. His face looks like a death mask. He holds the highest decoration given by the Soviet Union for heroism.
>
> One sunny March day he sent a bus for some of us staying in Kiev, two hours away. As we neared Chernobyl we sped over a road that is as clean as glass, for it is washed every other day. It goes mile after mile through deserted villages and farms and bleak, grey land that has been cleared of every sign of plant or animal life. The only movement comes from an occasional curtain blowing in an empty window. The thirty square

kilometer area that is Chernobyl itself is fenced and heavily guarded. From inside the gate the landscape looks like the outside – bare, flat and dotted with deserted houses and buildings. This had been a prosperous farming area until the worst nuclear disaster in history.

We changed into heavy brown protective uniforms, special boots and berets before being taken on a tour. I had read that Reactors 2 and 3 were still in operation producing the . . . energy which is carried out into the Ukraine by Chernobyl's many transmission towers; but it's a jolt to see them in operation right beside the tons of debris that is Reactor 4, buried in a mammoth concrete grave along with contaminated clothing, machinery and tools. How long will this be safe? I asked the same questions we are asking here at home [in the United States] where nuclear weapons plants are generating plutonium, an extraordinarily long-lived and toxic radioactive material, infinitely more dangerous to health and environment than the leftovers from a nuclear energy plant like Chernobyl. How long can that tomb . . . keep radioactive waste from leaking into the ground and aquifer?

Someone called these new friends of ours [the reactor engineering staff] the "John Wayne heros of the Soviet Union." They work 15 days at Chernobyl and then go home for 15 days. They retire at 50 if they live that long.

In this tragic wasteland, we were honored at a banquet (after washing in cold water and being scanned by Geiger counters). We filed into a formal dining room [and] after four courses and many non-alcoholic toasts to US–Soviet cooperation and to peace, I asked the chief scientist how long until another accident like this occurs somewhere in the world? "Ten years at most," was the answer. We didn't make any jokes on our way back to Kiev . . .

A particularly worrying problem, about which we know virtually nothing yet, is what the effect of radioactive contamination may be on soil bacteria. One distinguished physicist–ecologist has pointed out that if all human beings suddenly died then *Gaia*, the planet earth, would jog along with hardly a stumble. The natural and living "system" would receive a small, rather short input of rapidly putrefying protein, the worms would have a field day on many a sallow cheek, and then life would go on as usual. Perhaps even better without the Crazy Ape messing everything up by pouring toxic wastes into the air, oceans, rivers, and soil. Not a particularly flattering view of our own sense of importance, but uncomfortably true. But wipe out all soil bacteria, and the insects that breakdown cellulose in vegetation, and *Gaia* would be in real trouble, perhaps even mortally wounded as far as sustaining a total system supporting other forms of life.

It is for these reasons that we must learn as much as we possibly can from accidents of this sort, and this means putting into place, and sustaining over long years, monitoring programs and patient longitudinal studies. How many years? Possibly a century, at which point the caesium 137 will have decayed naturally to an eighth of what it is today, but who knows? As a human race we have never experienced anything like this before, not at Windscale, not at Three Mile Island. So we have to learn. As we shall see, there are certain things that we can do on a very limited geographical scale – say a few fields, a few square kilometers – but natural processes of decay, dilution and disconnection are really the only things we can rely on. And we know so little about these. Nearly all predictions about the natural removal of caesium contamination made during the first year have proved much too sanguine. Most of the predictions were based on mathematical equations which no one was quite sure about, equations often calibrated to quite different conditions than those to which they were applied. That is if they had been calibrated at all, and not just carried forward on the shoulders of a great mob of enthusiastic assumptions. "When in doubt, guess as well as you can" is a general rule that underpins many areas of scientific inquiry, but the guessing has to be honestly labelled as such, and then tested as rigorously and as soon as possible. Sometimes it is very difficult for scientists (except, almost by definition, the very best) to say "Sorry, I don't know," particularly when they are regarded as authorities, and become rather attached to the power and prestige that authority confers.

There is a human side to contamination too. All the people evacuated and exposed to levels of radiation exceeding the "allowable norms" (those controversial levels we shall have to think about very carefully later), now have a special medical card so that if they become ill at any time in the future doctors will know that they were involved with Chernobyl. Nearly 1 million people are in the monitoring programe, and 600,000 are being examined twice each year for any effects that could be ascribed to fallout and its radiation. In this way the largest long-term study in medical history has been set up, and assurances have been given that all data gathered over the years will be made freely available to the international community. At the moment, estimates of increased cancers vary widely, as much as a thousandfold, and scrupulous monitoring over many years is necessary to establish the facts.

Particular care and attention is being given to children and babies, including those who were still being carried by their mothers and born after the accident. In the earliest weeks of pregnancy there is conclusive evidence that even quite low levels of radiation, especially X-rays, can damage cell division. In the eighth to fifteenth week the problem becomes particularly acute, because it is then that the cells that will eventually make-up the brain separate out as a distinct mass in the growing embryo.

In the first year after the accident the Soviets carefully monitored more than 300 babies born to women in the most contaminated areas, but so far they report no signs of physical abnormalities. From prior experience about 26 cases of some mental retardation might be expected in a group of children this size, and estimates from Hiroshima victims lead doctors to suspect another 13 or so more might be detected. It is still too early to tell. As for older children, a few in rural areas with hot spots of fallout drank milk in the first few days, and their bodies concentrated the iodine 131 in their thyroid glands to give high doses. These children are also being monitored carefully, but generally the quick saturation of thyroid glands with potassium iodide tablets, and the strict regulation of milk, seem to have saved many children from chronic exposure.

Except in the first desperate hours of fire fighting, and during the days that followed in trying to put out the graphite fire, not many cared to volunteer to clean up the mess. Yet thousands were needed to carry out the decontamination plans, and military conscription for the dangerous duty was the only answer. The military were also the only group trained to handle decontamination problems because of the possibilities of atomic war. As is so often the case when unpleasant work has to be done, the finger of conscription from Moscow pointed not to White Russia, but to the small Baltic states of Estonia, Latvia, and Lithuania "incorporated" into the Soviet Union in 1945. It had been the same story in the early days of the Afghanistan invasion, when Latvians had been sent in among the first troops. Now young Estonian men in the army reserve were rounded up in the early hours of the morning without warning and summarily shipped to the Ukraine in a mood of "indignation, extreme bitterness and despair." The phrase appeared in the first of what was to be a series of newspaper articles published in Estonia after rumors of overexposure and radiation poisoning circulated. The conscripts were monitored for radiation exposure, but "volunteers" who entered Pripyat for one work shift received such doses that they were sent home to Estonia. Others, in zones farther from the reactor, were originally told that they had a two month duty, and went on strike when they were informed of an extension to six months. One Russian supervising a work squad made a macabre joke that a conjugal visit of an Estonian's wife was useless since the man was sterile by this time anyway. The journalist responsible for the articles wrote "Making strained jokes about relations between the sexes was like shaking a hornet's nest." The series of newspaper reports was stopped, but many in Estonia tune into television from Helsinki, just across the Gulf of Finland, and Estonians tend to be much better informed about the outside world than many in the Soviet Union. They quickly became aware of the international concern for something that could not be touched, tasted, heard, seen or smelled, an invisible presence that the body finally senses only when it is too late, when nausea and radiation sickness indicate exposure that only highly sensitive scientific instruments could have detected. The question is how do we detect and measure radiation in time? To answer that, we have to take our second of three "scientific and technical interludes."

7 How do we measure radiation?

All things in science are named and measured, even those things we cannot see. Or perhaps especially those things we cannot see – electrons, sounds, weights, temperatures, electric currents, wind velocities . . . and that Johnny-come-lately, radioactivity. To a large extent our simple knowing of the physical world depends upon our ability to design instruments that sense and measure the things we cannot measure with our own bodies. We extend and intrude ourselves out and into nature through the instruments we make. The radar beam caressing the thunderhead, the seismograph recording the earth's tremors, the electron microscope disclosing molecules, the telescope amplifying photons from the edge of the universe, the earth satellite disclosing the giant eddies of the Gulf Stream, the bubble chamber disclosing the track of an atomic particle – all these instruments are prosthetic devices whose ancestor is that simple measuring stick we call a ruler.

This is no accident. A ruler is a scale, something that we can see, and no matter how sophisticated and complex our instruments become the things they record must be translated ultimately into a light signal carrying a number to our eyes. We count things on "rulers" and then relate the numbers in various ways. That is all there is to Science. Not much when it is reduced to its essentials, but enough to let us say that most magical of human phrases "Oh, I see!" This is what we say when we suddenly understand, when something concealed from us in the darkness of our own ignorance comes into the light, when something *dawns* upon us. This is why for the ancient Greeks truth was *aletheia*, the prefix *a*-negating the concealing *Lethe*, the underworld, to make truth a lighting up, an un-concealment. To measure we need numbers and light for the sake of Truth.

A strange way to start a scientific and technical excursion? Not really. For we cannot sense radioactivity safely except through our eyes, by transforming it through an instrument to a number on a scale that we can read. The invisible that can kill has to be counted and made visible. The oldest way was to glue your eye to a small peephole in a box containing a metal and glass tube filled with a gas and an electrode at each end. When an atom split apart the particles ionized some of the gas atoms allowing an electrical current to jump the electrodes to produce a small flash of light. It was these flashes of light that Hans Geiger counted when he was a young research assistant to Ernest Rutherford at Cambridge, and they still lie behind the principle used today to observe and measure the existence of even smaller atomic particles – including those from outer space, with instruments weighing many tons buried deep in old mines. But Geiger got fed up crouching for hours with his eye to a small hole, counting the flashes of light as atoms decided to split. The photons of light that registered on his eye also made a slight "click" as the electric current passed, so by amplifying the sound one could sit back and count them. Hence the "Geiger counter," now a quite sensitive and sophisticated instrument conveniently packaged so you can hold it in your hand and take it out into the field.

Now counting clicks is all very well when you do not have too many atoms splitting up, but when many are fissioning away at once the pace of the clicks rises to a steady stream of sound so you can no longer distinguish and count the individual "atomic events." At this point you have to translate all those light flashes into a small voltage which moves a needle across a scale printed with numbers from which light can carry the numerical information to your eyes. So we are back to rulers and numbers again.

Today Geiger counters are not sensitive enough to measure many of the forms of radiation we want to know about; for example, the number of strontium 90 atoms spontaneously decaying in a leg of lamb, or the radioactive decay of caesium 137 in a trout. For more precise measurements instruments called scintillometers are used, but their name tells us that essentially the same principle is at work. Germanium or sodium iodide crystals are surrounded by very sensitive photoelectric cells, and when the gamma radiation released by a fissioning atom hits the crystal it "scintillates" – from the Latin *scintillare*, to twinkle or to emit sparks. The flashes of light in the crystal are counted as a small voltage, which moves a needle across a scale ... but you know where this ends now – rulers and numbers again.

With good instruments you would think it would be a relatively straightforward matter to measure radioactivity in a meaningful way. Well, yes and no, and the ambiguity comes from that little catch at the end – "in a meaningful way." The problem is that the discovery of radioactivity at the beginning of this century opened up all sorts of possibilities that had never been thought of before. Not just in physics and chemistry, but in medicine, biology, geology, archaeology, and a dozen other fields sensing and measuring radioactivity could now analyze the structure of matter, destroy a tumor, date a lava flow, and even provide evidence for the human presence itself – the ashes of a campfire on a cave floor leave behind their slowly decaying radionuclide carbon 14. The result of all these new possibilities was that people in various sciences tended to use measurements and scales and units that were the most convenient for them. And why not? Physicists are comfortable with *curies*, chemists grow up with *becquerels*, and when you add these up over time geneticists start to worry about *sieverts*, medical doctors are careful about their *grays*, and radiologists were probably introduced to *röntgens* – all names of men and women who have added to our understanding of radioactivity. Divide sieverts and grays by 100 and you have *rems* and *rads*, neither of which is easily convertible to each other because it depends on what sort of radiation one is talking about. The result is a scientific Tower of Babel, a cacophony of claims that one French report published by the nuclear power industry gaily called *une belle salade radioactive* – beautiful radioactive salad. Except that the units in the salad are measuring something whose consequences should have some human meaning. In the early days after Chernobyl even well-trained scientists from different backgrounds had great difficulty talking to each other, let alone providing a meaningful interpretation for journalists trying to make sense out of the "beautiful salad" for their readers. So what, rather precisely, is involved?

As we found out in our first technical excursion (pp. 3–9), when an atom of a radionuclide decays spontaneously it loses some of its energy in two ways. Some of the energy is carried away by pieces of the atom itself, either as alpha particles made up of two neutrons and two protons locked together, a form called alpha emission, or as single electrons or positrons, called beta emission. Compared to lightweight positrons and electrons, two neutrons and two protons bound together make up a very heavy particle carrying a considerable amount of energy. Like large calibre bullets at high speed, alpha particles can do a great deal of damage when they hit a target, and in assessing the potential danger to things like living cells alpha emissions are usually weighted 20 times the lighter beta sort.

Energy from a fissioning atom is also carried by gamma radiation, sometimes called gamma rays. These always travel at the speed of light and are like the X-rays used in hospitals except that they usually carry much more energy. So when we speak rather loosely about "radioactivity" we are really talking about the transmission of energy from a fissioning atom, either as waves of radiation, or by light or heavy particles moving at high speeds. Most of the energy disappears into space, or is absorbed by hitting things. The only time we really need to worry is when the things are alive, when the "things" are living cells in plants, animals, and you and me. When alpha and beta particles and gamma radiation slam into cells that are parts of us they can do considerable damage with their energy. Ultimately it all comes down to *energy*, so we shall have to start here and think about how we might measure it.

Take an electron and tie it down . . . well of course we cannot really do this, but we can carry out what a physicist would call a "thought experiment." Take an electron, which we know is negatively charged, and gradually bring an attracting positive charge near it until our straining electron "feels" one volt of potential. A volt of potential is just a small positive charge pulling our negative electron towards it, about the same voltage as you would feel if you put your tongue to small pieces of copper and zinc stuck in half a lemon. Now, like the hounds of Spring, we slip our electron from its traces. Free at last it accelerates towards the positive charge . . . and we are suddenly back 300 years with Sir Isaac Newton. It was he who defined a force as a mass (our tiny electron) multiplied by acceleration (the one volt of potential attraction). Like a tiny bullet our accelerated electron now carries the force or energy of an *electron volt* (eV), and this is going to form the basic unit in which we measure energy. It is a very small amount – one electron accelerated by the potential of half a lemon! – so we usually count in millions of electron volts, or mega electron volts (MeV). Depending upon the radionuclide, an alpha particle carries up to about 8 million electron volts (MeV), while a beta particle can get up to about 4 MeV. The energy carried by very high frequency gamma rays does not usually go beyond about 3 MeV.

We are almost there in our scientific and technical excursion, but not quite home yet. We know how to measure the energy of single alpha and beta particles, and the gamma radiation emitted from a fissioning atom, but the actual energy released by a radionuclide is going to depend on *how many* atoms decay spontaneously in a given time. If a radionuclide decays only one of its atoms every million years we are not going to hang around and bother to count it. It all comes down to how active a particular radionuclide is, and how often one of its atoms spontaneously fissions to release its energy. And so we have come at last to the basic unit we are going to use to measure radioactivity. We shall call one fissioning atom per second a *becquerel* (bq), our basic unit named after Antoine Becquerel, a Frenchman who investigated radioactivity at the end of the nineteenth century.

In reporting numbers of becquerels, or using them to measure radioactivity, we also have to tell people how much material we are referring to. For example, in many European countries and North America laws have been passed that forbid the sale of foods containing more than 300 becquerels of radioactivity *per kilogram* (2.2 pounds) for human consumption. But at this point we are getting close to the question of dosage, how much people may eat "safely," which depends on their eating habits

– how much they eat, what they eat, for how long, and a number of other things we shall have to think about later. This is a quite horrendously controversial area, one where scorn, derision, anger, accusation, and condescension rule, rather than quiet scientific discussion "for the sake of the truth." It is something we shall have to take up later in our third and final "scientific excursion," but for now we can simply say quite uncontroversially that 1 gram (a thousandth of a kilogram, or 0.0352 of an ounce) of plutonium 239 emits about 2 *billion* (2,000 million) alpha particles each second, in addition to lots of beta particles and gamma radiation. In other words, it does not take much plutonium in the environment before the becquerels of radioactive decay in meat, milk, and vegetables rise to totally unacceptable levels. In fact only about one-seven-millionth of a gram per kilogram (roughly two-billionths of an ounce per pound) of cauliflower or pork chops is needed, and after 24,000 years half of the stuff will still be emitting at the rate of 2 billion becquerels per gram. Not a very healthy thing to have around, and fortunately most of the plutonium 239 in nature has decayed over the roughly 4 billion years of the earth's lifetime to a scarcely measurable trace. The tens of thousands of kilograms now locked up in atomic bombs and nuclear fuel are all made by us. We have not only stolen fire from the gods, we are now creators ourselves. The Greeks called this *hubris*, and labelled it a dangerous game.

Now I realize that measuring radiation is not the most exciting of topics. It is technical, it requires concentration and effort, and only the most dedicated radiophysicist would pick up a text on measuring radioactivity as a bedside book before going off to sleep. But those cells bombarded by radiation may well be ourselves, or the cells of living things for which we have been granted the task of stewardship. Given what we have created, there is really no way we can take that sense of responsible caring seriously any more and remain ignorant of the most fundamental properties of radioactivity. At least we can measure it now with our basic unit the becquerel, the roughly 12–15 million electron volts of energy that are released each second as one atom of a radionuclide decays into its alpha, beta, and gamma components. What this means for living tissue depends on how much exposure the cells get, either in a quick flash or burst of energy, or accumulated over a long period of time. But this raises again the question of the meaning of dosage, which we shall take up later. For now we have enough to talk about radioactivity meaningfully, and it is time to see what happened to the radioactive air mass that exploded from Reactor 4, a cloud fed continuously for the next ten days with the largest amounts of radioactivity ever experienced outside of atomic bombs.

8   A cloud over Europe

The explosion that tore off the top of Reactor 4 blew an initial load of radionuclides 2 kilometers (about 1.5 miles) into the night sky, and the intense heat from the burning graphite core created a convection plume that continued to feed the great mass of radioactive air for the next ten days. What happened to that air mass in the first few days constitutes a meteorological detective story all on its own, a story pieced together by several computer models of atmospheric circulation that are usually run forwards to give us short-term weather predictions. This time they were first "run backwards" to locate the source of the radioactivity, and then run forwards to reproduce the main features of the path of the radioactive cloud as it dispersed over Europe. Later computer runs would track it over the entire northern hemisphere, tracks confirmed by many measurements on the ground.

The winds blowing the radioactive cloud around Europe were the result of a constantly shifting pattern of air pressure (figure 1), and at this point you really have to visualize a map of Europe drawn on a soft rubber sheet, pushed up here and there by tennis balls moving underneath to produce a shifting undulating surface. Any liquid, or in our case a radioactive air mass, would move to and fro according to the shape of the constantly heaving surface. We see the effects of such pressure surfaces every night on television during the weather news when successive snapshots taken from weather satellites are linked together to show the shifting cloud patterns. During April 25, the day the spindown test was being planned, there was a center of high pressure over northeastern Russia, with a smaller, much more local high beginning to form over Germany. Between them was a trough of low pressure pointing straight from the Ukraine northwest to the Baltic and Scandinavia through northeastern Poland.

You would think intuitively that winds would run straight down "hills" of high air pressure to the low "valleys" or troughs, rather like water finding the shortest path as it runs in brooks and rills down a hillside. This would mean that winds blowing on Chernobyl would come from the high pressure zone over the northeast and blow southwest at right angles into the trough over southern Poland, Czechoslovakia,

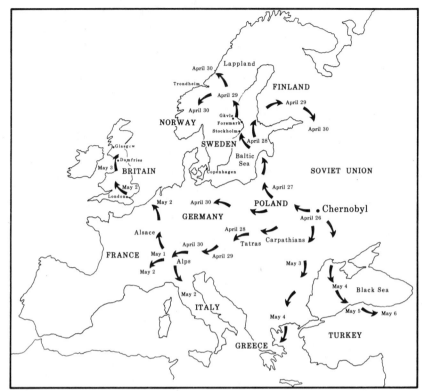

Figure 1 The general movement of the radioactive emissions from Chernobyl, realizing that it is difficult to capture a highly dynamic movement of airmasses over 10 days in a single static map.

Hungary, and Romania. But this is where our intuition and water analogy breaks down, because we have not taken into account the actual spin of the earth, the so-called Coriolis effect.

As the earth spins it also imparts a force to the air masses travelling over its surface, tending to curl them clockwise in the northern hemisphere and anti-clockwise in the southern hemisphere. There is literally a rule of thumb you can use to remember this which is particularly useful if you are right-handed and are holding something like a pencil or a book. Using your left hand make a "thumbs-up" sign, point your index finger forward like a pistol, and stick your second finger out at right angles to it. Then in the northern hemisphere (thumb up), the wind (index finger) is curled to the right (second finger). If you are in the southern hemisphere point your thumb down with the other fingers still at right angles and the rule still works. If you happen to be left-handed, bad luck – you have to reverse it all. No one said life was simple. I have even caught meteorologists surreptitiously using this rule of thumb to remind themselves, although I look the other way in order not to embarrass them.

So winds blowing out of the high pressure zone over Russia were now curled or twisted to the right, blowing parallel and straight through the low pressure trough that acted as a meteorological funnel carrying much of the radioactivity northwest.

Who actually detected the radioactivity first outside of the Soviet Union and sounded the alarm is a moot point, but what is certain is that Poland actually did detect it and did not realize it at first. During the early evening of April 27, about 41 hours after the first explosion, an operator at Mikolajki in northeastern Poland, one of the country's 140 permanent radiological measuring stations, went out to check the reading. The instrument registered 700 times the normal background level, and the operator simply said "O cholera, ta jebana wskazowka znow sie zacciela!," roughly "Oh hell, the damned needle's stuck again." He took it inside, cleaned and dusted it, and then replaced it in the dark. The next morning he read the instrument again, saw the needle was still lurching off the end of the scale, and realized that more than a bit of dust was involved. At nine o'clock he picked up the telephone to the Laboratory for Radiation Protection at Warsaw, whose director immediately ordered him to go on an emergency footing, replacing the air filters every 2 hours and reporting the results at once. Other stations in eastern Poland were put on a similar emergency schedule, and by the next day all 140 stations in the country were reporting on a continuous basis. Fortunately there was little rain over Poland at the time, so most of the initial radioactive cloud passed through.

The radioactivity recorded in the air by the monitoring stations was not only from the fine particles deposited on the filters; there was also some gamma radiation from large quantities of highly radioactive xenon 133, krypton 85 and other noble gases which together accounted for as much radiation as all the other elements – about 40 of them combined. Discharges of noble gases are seldom mentioned or taken into account because they are usually inert, combining with other elements only under very special, and only recently discovered, chemical and physical conditions. For this reason, and because they eventually become highly diluted through turbulent mixing in the atmosphere, they are often ignored. But when a large and still concentrated "packet" of radioactive noble gases sweeps through an area its gamma radiation can be extremely dangerous even though it does not become mechanically attached or chemically combined with body tissues.

What was not realized at the time of the first alarms, and perhaps could only have been seen in the clear light of hindsight, was that Poland had actually received and recorded a warning of a large explosion only minutes after the accident at Chernobyl. Seismologists in Warsaw, checking the instruments recording small quakes and tremors, were able to detect a highly distinctive "double wave" at the time of the accident, a waveform that is the signature of a sharp explosion, perhaps an underground atomic test, rather than an earthquake. If this small signal had been interpreted at the time, and cross checked with other seismic stations, the "epicenter" of the explosion at Chernobyl could have been pinpointed within the hour. But who watches for faint double waves at two o'clock in the morning?

Others may also have known about the explosion and fire very early on. Military satellites are constantly scanning the earth, and their technical capability is far superior to the low resolution instruments available to civilians and scientists. If the white lines on parking lots could be photographed by U2 overpass flights at 25,000 meters (80,000 feet) in the 1960s, it does not take much imagination to think about the capability of satellite surveillance in the 1980s. Every time a spacecraft is propelled into space with a white hot rocket engine it is recorded by American and Soviet intelligence satellites. It is rumored that any time a tank hiding in a Czechoslovakian or French forest switches on its engine the infrared radiation generated is recorded somewhere as a white spot on a monitoring screen. So why was an intense graphite fire throwing visible and infrared radiation into space not picked up and immediately reported? Either the instruments are pathetically inadequate, or the event was in fact recorded. That it was not reported immediately raises ethical questions that must trouble anyone who stands in the tradition that answers "yes" to the question "Am I my brother's keeper?"

At about the same time that Warsaw was beginning to realize something was up, workers on the night and day shifts were changing at the Forsmark atomic power station on the Baltic coast of eastern Sweden just north of Stockholm. Monitoring radioactivity continuously is required at all atomic plants in Sweden and the gates are watched by highly sensitive scintillation counters. As workers came to the building and crossed the open ground to the gates of the plant they picked up radioactive particles on their shoes. It was these minute specks that triggered the alarm. At first a malfunction and leak at Forsmark were suspected, and the whole plant was evacuated except for a skeleton staff that stayed on duty to run and check the reactors. The problem was that no one could find anything wrong, and soon people realized that a new and strongly detectable source of radioactivity was literally all around them. The Radiological Protection Board in Stockholm was informed at ten o'clock that morning, and an emergency meeting held only a half an hour later. Very quickly other reports began coming in: from a research center at Studsvik on the coast south of Stockholm, from Sweden's three other power plants, from the Finnish Center for Radiation and Nuclear Safety, and an atmospheric research station at Risø in Denmark. By one o'clock in the afternoon, and only 45 minutes after being alerted, Sweden's National Defense Research Institute was able to calculate the trajectories of the air mass arriving in Sweden's eastern border and pinpoint a radioactive source "somewhere in the Ukraine." During the afternoon and evening special Lansen jet aircraft took air samples from 300 meters above the cold waters of the Baltic up to 12 kilometers in the troposphere, and a marine helicopter equipped with a highly sensitive germanium scintillometer was filling in the details. By evening Sweden's meteorological service had pinpointed Chernobyl, and Sweden's ambassador in Moscow was making strong representations for full information. By any standards it was an enormously impressive national and scientific effort conducted under the most urgent and stringent circumstances. What warning Europe had was due largely to these Swedish efforts, helped by confirming reports from neighboring countries.

Some of these confirming reports came from Finland, even though the initial response had been much less certain. During the Sunday evening, as Polish instruments were being dusted off, a heavy shower of rain at Kajaani in southern Finland had brought down a little of the fallout at the leading edge of the Chernobyl cloud. After leaving Poland, and while over the Baltic, the air currents had diverged, the lower ones containing most of the fallout swinging west towards Sweden, while the upper levels carrying somewhat less continued to curl east to Finland. While Finland eventually received considerable fallout, the initial amounts were so small that they might have been caused by the snow melting in the spring giving up minute amounts of radon gas released by radioactive materials from previous atomic bomb tests. This sort of slight increase in activity had been observed before, so no one reacted very strongly to the first weak signs. Only the next day, as the Forsmark results started coming through, were all the other monitoring stations put on an emergency status to report their readings every hour.

It quickly became apparent, even in these first few days, that rainfall was going to be the big problem. This was well known in the Soviet Union and was the reason low cumulus clouds approaching the Ukraine were dispersed by seeding with silver iodide crystals. Providing the radioactive air was relatively dry, the usual case with winds from high pressure areas being compressed and heated, all was well. Most of the larger radioactive particles had fallen out closer to the source over the

Ukraine, and only relatively small ones remained suspended. A small proportion of these continued to drift slowly down, but the ground contamination was relatively slight. But let a warm dry air mass from the south meet a cool moisture laden packet at a "front" and you have real trouble on your hands. The advancing front of cool moist air forces the warmer air aloft, cools it and mixes with it in a very turbulent fashion, and down comes the rain picking up and scavenging most of the radioactive particles still held in suspension. This is exactly what happened over central and northern Sweden and central Norway as a wedge of cooler moist air pushed eastward from the north Atlantic to produce some of the heaviest fallout and contamination outside of the Soviet Union. We shall look at this in some detail later as we take up the plight of Norway and Sweden and the far reaching effects of the radioactivity.

Meanwhile over the Baltic the wedge of cold air from the Atlantic continued to move slowly eastward distorting the trough channelling the radioactive air to Scandinavia, and beginning to block its forward motion. Thwarted in their northwesterly run, the winds now blew southwest carrying the radioactivity in a great tongue over eastern Europe, Germany, Austria, Italy, Switzerland, and France. If the air had not been fed continuously by the heat plume at Chernobyl, and if rain had not fallen, all might have been reasonably well. The fine radioactive particles might have been held in suspension until the cloud mixed and dispersed after encountering cooler air over the ocean.

Unfortunately, contaminated packets of air do not rise only when they meet other, denser air masses. Mountains also force them aloft, and cool them off, and . . . down comes the rain. On April 30 and May 1 a great swath of deposition was scavenged by the rain over Austria, Switzerland, southern Germany, northern Italy and southern France, the great alpine chain of Europe that points towards the High Tatra and Carpathian Mountains of eastern Czechoslovakia and southern Poland. But by this time the warning had been given, and even the Soviets had produced their terse three sentence announcement. It would be another week, after the fire had been extinguished, before any details were known, but thanks to Sweden's efforts the radioactive cat was very much out of the Chernobyl bag by this time and all of Europe was on the alert. Austria already had a dense network of 320 monitoring stations in place, and was able to record the growing intensity of the fallout on an hour by hour basis. There were certainly concentrations and hot spots in the lowland areas of the Danube, but by far the greatest contamination fell on the upper slopes and high summer pastures of the Alps.

Just to the west, at the University of Konstanz in southern Germany, the faculty of the physics department had with them a remarkable colleague on sabbatical leave from the United States. He had been deeply concerned for many years about the effects of radioactivity, and his testimony had been instrumental in stopping atomic tests in Alaska in the 1960s. These would have been conducted "in places where it didn't matter" by people who were apparently oblivious that there might be "side effects" if atomic bombs were used for large scale engineering purposes. Ever since those days he had been in the habit of carrying a small Geiger counter when he travelled and routinely switching it on each morning.

On the morning of April 30, five days after the accident, the needle did not quiver slightly to measure the normal background radiation, but went clear off the scale, signalling that the Chernobyl cloud had arrived. In a concerted and public spirited effort, many of the faculty and students in the physics department started to monitor the fallout and to conduct a series of important experiments over the next few weeks. We shall look at some of these a little later, but it was already clear that rainfall held the key. As soon as the radioactive air hit a mountain barrier the clouds condensed, often as thunderheads with highly local rainfall. Areas around Konstanz recorded up to 250,000 becquerels per square meter (bq/m²) on the ground, while only 100 kilometers away at Stuttgart less than 15,000 bq/m² were recorded.

The swath of contaminated air continued southwest, with high levels of fallout over the Swiss Alps, and arrived over eastern France on April 30, peaking on May 2. All this was known by the French government whose spokesmen quite deliberately lied to the French people. According to the official version, it was as though the ghost of de Gaulle had risen at the French border, raising his hands against the cloud and saying "It shall not pass!" Only on May 10, when calf thyroids with 2,600 bq/kg, eaten as sweetbreads in Alsace, were taken off the market, did the French people realize that "doing a Verdun" was not the effective way to deal with this invisible enemy. It is worth noting that France relies on nuclear power more than any other country in the world, something we shall touch upon again.

Now another shift in the undulating air pressure surface came, and the tongue of air that had licked the Alpine peaks swung north over Belgium, Holland, and Britain. Once again rain was the problem. Relatively little contamination fell out over low lying areas, but the hills and mountains of Wales, Cumbria (the Lake District) and the Highlands of Scotland all received heavy loads of caesium 134 and 137, as well as the shorter lived iodine 131. Over 68,000 bq/m² were recorded in Cumbria, and 21 days later sheep grazing on the grass had 240,000 bq/kg in their thyroids. Over the rest of Europe fickle winds continued to scatter the air mass, a mass now being fed increasingly by a partly smothered but very hot reactor. Even now we know few details about the situation in the Eastern bloc countries of Europe, because Romania, Czechoslovakia, and Bulgaria reported nothing before May 5–8, and even then in the most guarded and noncommittal terms. What few readings we have were made by people at the American Embassy in Bucharest. Greece had already started recording increased levels by May 2, peaking on May 5, although no announcement was made by the government until the next day. But four Greek children tested later in the Massachusetts General Hospital had high levels of iodine 131 in their thyroid glands, and we now know (three years later) that these measurements are distressingly symptomatic of the situation over much of eastern Europe. But from this part of the world there is only silence, or reassuring bureaucratic noises.

On May 5, ten days after the accident, the hoses of liquid nitrogen were forced into the reactor building at Chernobyl, and at last the fires were extinguished. No longer fed by the radioactive plume, the shifting winds dispersed the remaining contamination, some of it falling in minute amounts as far away as Japan and the western United States. But the patchwork quilt of radioactive contamination it produced over Europe left behind widespread fear. After all, if this was up to one million times the discharge of Three Mile Island then what did it mean for you and me and the children? In those early days the collective angst coefficient of Europe rose with every becquerel reported. And who could you trust anyway? The scientists who said it could not happen? The governments who accepted the experts' advice? Two questions were on everyone's lips. The first was "What shall we do?" and the second was "What does it all mean?" In particular, what does it mean to be exposed to all those becquerels, whether eaten or drunk as food, or inhaled in the air? At this point we have to make our final scientific and technical excursion, an excursion to answer a question probably more fraught with controversy than almost any other today as doctors and scientists debate how safe is "safe?"

9 How much radiation is safe?

As we start this final scientific and technical excursion let me give you a full, frank, and fair warning. We are entering an area of great dispute marked by much tension, an area where few express any doubts one way or another, where the no-man's-land between opposing sides is so narrow that few have either the room or the courage to stand there taking the scornful disparagement and moral accusations that are hurled at them from either side. If you ever thought science was a cool and detached search for the objective truth, an enterprise cloistered from the self-serving hubbub of daily life, this account should do much to change your mind. I can think of no area of science today where the prior intellectual commitments and stances so strongly shape the interpretations placed on scientific "texts," or allow such unwarranted extrapolations from assumptions grounded in ignorance. If you are pronuclear (power or bombs), you will accuse me of uninformed hyperbole at best, and outrageous dissimulation, distortion and downright lying at worst. If you are antinuclear, you will point to my distressing lack of moral fiber, my abandonment of all ethical responsibility to future generations, my failure of nerve to make a righteous commitment to truth.

But I call myself a Professor, and I must try in my own imperfect human way to profess the truth as I can grasp it at this moment. Equally important, I must profess openly that I do not know what the truth may be. Such a whimper of ignorance may not engender feelings of robust confidence, but it is, when all is said and done, the small quiet voice that drives science forwards. And there are, fortunately, still men and women in science today, perhaps the very best, who are prepared to stand in that rather lonely inbetween world and say, "I don't know . . . but in the name of the gods who have fled let us find out."

Many of them are in universities protected by academic tenure from the exercises of power that try to remove opposition or attempt to cover up a truth that raises proper doubts. That is why authoritarian states and institutions revoke or discourage academic tenure (as in Britain today), so that unruly scholars seeking awkward truths may be disciplined. In fact such threats are seldom needed for much more subtle ways are available and are too often effective. Research on radiation just happens not to be funded; reviewers of scientific proposals disparage research questions whose answers might conflict with their own preconceptions; "If Pennsylvania does not accept a low radiation disposal site it will lose $700,000 in Federal funds;" public documents are marked "Confidential" and withheld from the public; "Go and ask the university scientists, they are not as restricted as we are" ... and so on. We shall meet such instances and many more in the pages that follow. I will do my best to explain and to lay out what is known and what is not known, but you must read carefully and come to your own conclusions. Or, if you really cannot stand "all that technical stuff" you can skip over this, but I think you owe it to yourself to try. That cell knocked askew by radiation may belong to you.

Remember (p. 35) that radiation really comes down to energy, to alpha and beta particles and gamma radiation carrying energy away from a fissioning atom. The question is, what is energy? This is a very difficult question embedded in the old Greek word *energeia* used by Aristotle as he tried to think about things and how they move. Most scientists today are not given to such philosophical reflections, preferring to put "all that metaphysical stuff" aside and get on with the job. Getting on with the job usually means finding a satisfactory definition that works, an operational (*opus*, work) definition that forms a starting point. So in a rather prosaic way we shall define a unit of energy as the work we have to do to accelerate a mass of 1 gram 1 centimeter in 1 second, and call this amount of work or energy an *erg*. It is not very much: take a small gram weight, about 0.035 of an ounce, and push it with your finger 1 centimeter in 1 second. Most of the work you do, most of the ergs you burn up on such an exercise, will be used in moving several thousands of grams of muscle and bone in your arm, hand, and fingers. Or, to go to the other extreme, to accelerate a 908,000 gram (2,000 pound) sports car from 0 to 2,675 centimeters per second (60 mph) in 5.4 seconds, you would need to apply something like 449,460,000 ergs of energy each second to the driving wheels – ignoring wind resistance, road slippage, and all the other imperfections of a real experiment.

Now alpha and beta particles are not sports cars or even gram weights, but belong to the minute world of atoms. A becquerel (bq) is one atom splitting per second to release about 15 million electron volts (MeV), which may sound a lot but is only about 0.000024 of an erg. It would take 19,000,000,000,000 (19 trillion) becquerels to accelerate our sports car, but it is already obvious that we shall have to do something about all those zeros. From now on we will write these numbers scientifically, so that 19 trillion becomes 19×10^{12} (the 12 telling us the number of zeros after the 19), and the 0.000024 ergs will be 24×10^{-6} (the -6 letting us know the number of places we have to move the decimal point to the left). Our concern for radiation arises because the energy released by atoms is absorbed by living things. For example, 1 gram of radium gives out 37 billion (or 37×10^9) becquerels, an amount that an older way of measuring radiation called one *curie*. If you held this in your hand for 1 second you would receive about 16 times a fatal dose of radiation. Except for the flash of an atomic bomb, or the intense exposure received by the men in the reactor room at Chernobyl, most people are not suddenly exposed to these huge amounts but to much smaller quantities over longer periods of time. Madame Curie herself died of radiation exposure because she worked with radium compounds over many years. This means that to compute doses we have to add up all the smaller amounts over time. A scientist would say we are "integrating over time" to give the *absorbed dose*, the amount of energy actually absorbed by a piece of bone, muscle, thyroid gland, kidney, or whole human body. So absorbed doses are measured and stated as "so much energy (ergs) absorbed by so much matter (grams)."

If 1 gram of your tissue receives 10,000 ergs of energy from radiation the absorbed dose is called a *gray*. If you divide this by 100, to get 100 ergs per gram, the absorbed dose is called a *rad* for *r*adiation *a*bsorbed *d*ose. You can see that underneath all this terminology are some very simple and straightforward ideas expressed in the arithmetic we all learned in elementary school. As we shall see, the difficulties arise not from what we know and measure and add up, but from what we do not know as we try to give meaning to the measurements and the arithmetic.

Grays and rads were early measures in radiation medicine, but they are used less today in studies of human beings and animals. We now realize that it makes a considerable difference to living cells whether energy is carried by alpha or beta particles or by gamma radiation. With their relatively large mass alpha particles are particularly energetic, so their effect on living tissue is usually weighted 20 times that of the beta and gamma energies, even though alpha particles do not penetrate very far (about 1 millimeter, so the already dead skin cells on your hands called calluses will absorb them). However, when a radionuclide like caesium 137 is inhaled or ingested there are thousands of living cells within those small spheres of 1 millimeter radius surrounding each fissioning particle. To take these differences into account we simply weight the absorbed dose by the type of energy (alpha, beta, or gamma) to compute something called the *absorbed dose equivalent* measured in *sieverts* (Sv). This unit is named after the Swedish physicist Rolf Sievert, a major figure in studies on the effects of radiation on people and other living things. If we are talking about energy from fissioning radionuclides, then sieverts are just weighted grays, and the 10,000 ergs per gram of a gray are now equivalent to 111,333 ergs per gram of one sievert (see appendix, p. 151). Divide a sievert by 100 and you have a *rem*, standing for radiation equivalent *m*an, although unfortunately it applies to women and children too.

It is also possible to take into account the parts of the body exposed. Ovaries and testes are considered the most vulnerable because of the effect of radiation on chromosomes and their genetic structure, but breast, lung, and marrow tissue are also weighted heavily. As different radionuclides are absorbed differentially into the body a doctor or health physicist may take these things into account to calculate an *effective dose equivalent*. This is why, for example, strontium 90 is so dangerous, because it is taken up into the bone where its damage to the marrow making blood corpuscles may be especially severe. For most calculations, however, we usually stop at the dose equivalent and compute sieverts.

What happens when someone eats or drinks food that has been contaminated by Chernobyl fallout? The absorbed dose equivalent they actually receive depends on three things. First, the sheer number of becquerels ingested, the number of spontaneous emissions per second within the human body. Second, the rates at which various radionuclides are absorbed by the body. These rates depend on whether the radionuclides are in relatively soluble forms, easily moved from the lung and stomach to other parts of the body, like the thyroid gland, kidneys, bones, and muscles, or in relatively insoluble forms that pass through the stomach to be eliminated quite quickly. The International Commission on Radiological Protection (ICRP) continues to publish and update extremely detailed reports that are based on every scrap of reliable knowledge available at the time. For example, about 10 percent of strontium 90 is absorbed, but virtually all of the caesium 134 and 137 ingested moves quickly from the stomach to muscle tissue.

Finally, the actual dose received will also depend on how long the radionuclides spend in the body. Each one has not only a physical halflife, but also a biological halflife, the time the body takes to get rid of half of the source of radioactivity it has absorbed. For example, strontium 90 has a biological halflife in bone of about 50 years, which is why even small amounts can be so dangerous. Once the body absorbs it into the skeletal structure it is virtually there for a person's lifetime. In contrast, caesium 137 has a biological halflife of 70 days, so after a couple of years, roughly 700 days, it has virtually disappeared from the muscles.

Taking radiation rates, absorption rates, and rates of biological halflife into account complicates the bookkeeping arithmetic considerably, but health physicists have worked out very good "rules of thumb" that can quickly translate becquerels ingested each day into the sieverts of absorbed dose equivalents. In the case of caesium 137, for example, one becquerel is equivalent to 1.3×10^{-8} Sv. This means that if you ingested 300 bq each day for a year you would absorb a dose equivalent of:

$$300 \text{ bq} \times 1.3 \times 10^{-8} \times 365 \text{ days} = 1.424 \times 10^{-3} \text{ Sv}$$
$$\text{or } 1.424 \text{ millisieverts (mSv)}$$

In a rather frustrating way, particularly after that arithmetic, this cannot mean anything to us at the moment because we have yet to take up the question of limits and what is dangerous. But to be honest to ourselves we have got to get the arithmetic right first.

Is this, in fact, the dose that someone consuming 300 bq of Chernobyl fallout each day for a year would receive? The answer is actually "no" for a couple of reasons. First, and depending very much on where you live, the natural background radiation from cosmic rays, traces of radionuclides in the natural environment, radon gas from decaying uranium, and so on may give an annual dose of 2–5 mSv. Sometimes it may be much higher when, for example, people in eastern Pennsylvania build their houses on an intruded dyke of rock containing uranium ore. Many tend to shrug their shoulders about background radiation, but we realize now that we can do something about it. Better sealing and ventilation of basements can reduce radon, often the biggest component of background radiation, and if we are sensible we do not make cement block out of uranium mine tailings as some did in Colorado. There is an unfortunate "mental shrugging" attitude to background radiation, especially when man-made radiation like Chernobyl fallout is compared to it. The problem here is that fallout tends to accumulate in many more specific places in the body and to a higher degree than most background radiation, and the accumulations place that heavily weighted alpha radiation right next to lung, stomach, and muscle cells. We should think very hard and carefully before we shrug off any form or source of radiation. Most natural radionuclides have a much smaller chance of entering the body because they seldom get into the foodchain. Secondly, 300 bq from caesium 137 means another 150 bq from caesium 134 if we are talking about Chernobyl fallout, plus some ruthenium and other traces. Our first calculation of 1.424 mSv should be increased to about 2.136 mSv, at least during the first couple of years.

Unfortunately there are still many gaps in our knowledge that have nothing to do with the simple bookkeeping arithmetic, particularly when it comes to direct and practical matters concerning living things. For example, a number of careful studies working with lambs and ewes had established the rate at which the radioactivity in grass contaminated with caesium was transferred as becquerels into muscle tissue. This "transfer coefficient," the rate at which the transformation from grass to flesh takes place, is obviously very important if you are raising sheep for market and people are eating the meat. The problem was that the early studies were carried out in lowland pastures around the Sellafield nuclear power plant in northwestern England, and these had established a transfer coefficient of about 10–20 percent – 2,000 bq in a day's feed became transformed to 200–400 bq per kilogram of meat. But when sheep were fed on upland pasture the transfer coefficient jumped to nearly 80 percent. Now 2,000 bq in the daily intake of grass became 1,600 bq/kg, well above the levels allowed for human consumption. What worked for one very carefully calibrated situation gave completely false and misleading results in another. If we can think of anything good coming out of Chernobyl it is that we have an unprecedented opportunity to learn as much as we possibly can from this huge "experiment," and so will have more knowledge to deal with the next disaster.

But now it comes: we have to enter this most controversial of areas, the actual human meaning of all the bookkeeping arithmetic. Here we hit questions like "What level of radiation is safe?," "Is there a safe level?," and even "What do you mean by safe?" These are questions whose answers mean many different things to different people. Even if people agree more or less on the straightforward facts of the numbers and the arithmetic, these numerical statements or "texts" may still be interpreted quite differently and be given quite different meanings. It turns out that how people perceive, assess and interpret risks is not something that can be detached from the cultural matrix in which those people are embedded. And when I say "cultural matrix" I really mean the particular "intellectual situations" in which people find themselves, the slowly changing structures of thinking that characterize all of us. As children we are all thrown into a world not of our own making, we are shaped by that world, and later we begin to shape it for ourselves and for others to some degree. If you care about the issues in this book, then when you have finished it, and have reflected carefully upon these things, your "world" will have changed somewhat whether you agree or disagree. A man or woman coming to these matters from the purely calculative world of the statistician will place one interpretation on the facts – if they can be established. And statisticians do try to establish facts of a certain kind with a certain degree of confidence. But a doctor, nuclear power manager, investor, farmer, young mother, fisherman, ecologist, government official . . . all will bring their own "worlds" to bear on the "numerical text" and may well interpret the text differently because their "worlds" carry both different preconceptions and different moral values.

There, I have said it. Moral values: what we believe is "meet and right," what is decent, and just and good and prudent. In the midst of science we need philosophers as perhaps we never needed them before. Let no one ever persuade you that these are questions to which there is one clear and objective scientific meaning leading to one clear and objective scientific answer. As a matter of fact sometimes even the text, the scientific facts, may not be that clear, so we are all trying to interpret things that are still somewhat obscure and seen through a glass darkly.

"Well for heaven's sake," you might expostulate, "Surely we have enough evidence today that radiation is harmful?" And the answer is once again one of those exasperating yes and nos. The problem is that at relatively high levels of exposure to radiation we know a fair amount, not as much as we would like, but enough to make any normal, non-suicidal person very frightened and take every precaution possible to avoid it. Hiroshima and Nagasaki stand as terrible monuments to the human horror of intense radioactivity, and so do the lives of the poor souls on small islands in the South Pacific drenched with fallout from atomic bomb tests. There are also meticulous epidemiological studies of people who had a terrible disease of the spine treated with very heavy doses of X-rays, and we use radiotherapy daily to kill rapidly proliferating cells in cancerous tumors. There is no need to establish the effects of such high radiation any more, and they are not in dispute.

What is far less well established, and what causes enormous disagreement and great tension, is the effects of low radiation, especially over relatively long periods of time, although we have to be extremely careful about short exposures too under certain circumstances. One of the most distinguished figures in radiation epidemiology discovered highly detrimental effects from even a single X-ray photograph on the fetus inside a mother's womb, especially if what was once thought to be a perfectly safe dose of radiative energy was delivered during the early stage of development. This was during the time when the cells that were ultimately going to become brain tissue were beginning to separate out from the mass of cells making up the minute embryo. The Oxford Survey of Childhood Cancers stands as a major and undisputed accomplishment in the field today, and although it was vigorously challenged, disparaged and denigrated at the time, no responsible doctor would take such X-rays today. It is worth noting that over the past 50 years what has been considered a "safe dose" has been constantly lowered as we learn more and more about the long-term effects of radiation.

No, the problem is not the effects of high radiation doses, but what happens when low doses are encountered. The big fear is cancer, when the energy from radioactivity damages cells, either turning them cancerous, or doing genetic damage to sperm or ovum so that either deformed children result, or they themselves carry defective genes down to future generations. At these lower levels we cannot say "50 millisieverts and you will get cancer," but only "50 millisieverts and there is such-and-such a chance that you will develop some sort of cancer as a result." We are in that difficult, always controversial and gray area of probability. The nub of the problem is that "such-and-such chance," and how we estimate it in a sure and reliable way.

At the moment we cannot, and I shall state our lack of precise knowledge flatly without any ifs, buts, or other qualifications. At this moment, and despite all the confident noises made by scientists offstage, I do not think we know for sure. The scientists have their preconceptions too, some of them fully justified on good scientific or moral grounds – and sometimes both. But we are getting closer to more reliable answers, although it is patient work, and likely to be distressingly long too. The problem is that we cannot in all human conscience run an experiment here. To do so would put us straight back in the moral category of the Nazis who carried out ghastly experiments with concentration camp victims during the Second World War. You cannot design experiments with people all nicely standardized and controlled for age, health and sex, and then expose them to different amounts of radiation for different amounts of time and follow them up over 50 years to see what you can say about the probabilities at the end of it all – not if the word "civilization" has any meaning left. What we can do today, given the sheer fact of Chernobyl, is monitor the very large number of people exposed, and then try to learn more from the unplanned "experiment" that suddenly appeared in our midst. This is why it is so terribly important that the Soviet Union continues its new policy of openness, and shares all its growing epidemiological knowledge about Chernobyl with the rest of the world.

The problem is that we do not know exactly how to extrapolate back from high radiation doses and high probabilities of cancer to the region of low doses. And by "region" I mean literally an area on a piece of graph paper (figure 2) on which we try to fit the best curve to the current information we have about doses and cancers. In the top right hand corner of high doses and high probabilities we have quite a lot of information, and we can try out a number of different curves, all of which fit reasonably well and only tell us the obvious anyway; namely, do not mess around with high radiation. Whether a high dose gives a 50 or 60 percent chance of a cancerous death is beside the point for most people, and we do not need any fancy curvefitting to tell us that.

But any curvefitting we do in that top right hand corner leaves us a long "tail" flapping down there in the lower left hand corner, and that is

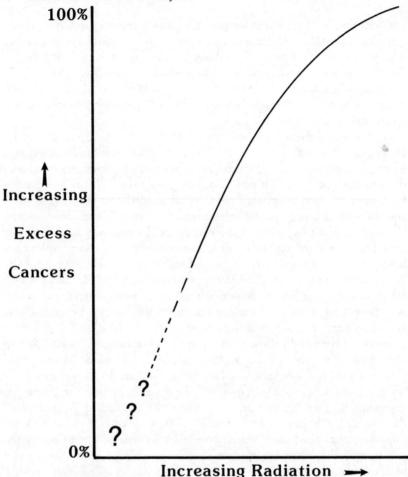

Figure 2 Plotting increasing radiation against excess deaths from cancers (deaths over and above those expected from other causes). At high levels of radiation we know excess deaths increase rapidly (top right hand corner), but at low radiation levels there is much controversy.

precisely where we are the most ignorant. So let us enlarge that lower corner (figure 3) and see what the possibilities are. If our vertical axis is measuring the probability of excess cancers – cancers over and above those normally expected according to current rates – then we might ask whether really minute doses of radiation have any effect at all. This would imply that we were on Curve A, which only starts to rise after a certain threshold value has been reached. I do not think any responsible scientist holds to this idea today in the face of the evidence we now have. As the

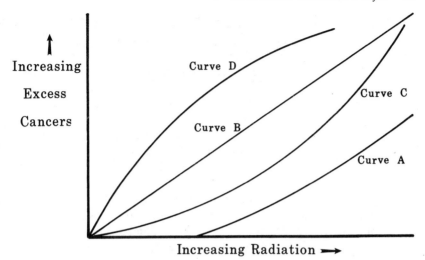

Figure 3 Some of the possible relationships between low levels of radiation and excess deaths from cancer.

Oxford Survey demonstrated, even minute amounts of radiation can damage a cell, and perhaps the very lowest energy level we should consider is that which can break a molecular bond. This is far below the energy released by a single fissioning atom, so it is reasonable to discount Curve A as a possibility. Even the smallest amount of radiation is going to increase the chances slightly, meaning any curve we use must start rising from a point essentially indistinguishable from zero.

So another possibility is Curve B, the so-called "linear hypothesis," which simply says our best guess is that the probability of cancer rises in direct proportion to the dose. For many years quite a lot of scientists, many of them from the atomic power industry, or strongly supportive of it, thought this was a curve that actually overestimated the chance of cancer. They preferred to believe in Curve C rather than B, although there was precious little hard evidence for either. They rather magnanimously granted those who did not agree with them that they would condescendingly accept the conservative linear hypothesis "for the sake of argument," implying that the risks were so small anyway that it did not make much difference. Perhaps you can already feel the way "worlds" and their preconceptions inform the questions and interpretations?

But slowly and patiently the harder evidence is being gathered, much of it through the extremely careful and detailed work of people associated with the original Oxford Survey, only this time they have used data over a period of 33 years about people who worked in the Hanford plant in the US state of Washington making plutonium 239 for atomic weapons. As a result of this work there is growing evidence that something like Curve D fits the known facts best of all. This work has been published in a scientifically refereed medical journal, and was also put forward at an extensive inquiry on low level radiation effects in and around a large atomic plant (Sizewell) in eastern Britain. Significantly, at a similar inquiry on Windscale (Sellafield) in northwestern England seven years earlier, the same sort of testimony had been virtually dismissed in the final report. However, this time a distinguished member of Britain's National Radiation Protection Board (NRPB), who had also been one of the scientific assessors at the Sellafield inquiry, said "I believe the evidence she produced is sound ... and if her data had not been scrutinized they might have been dismissed." If Curve D is correct, and it does fit the facts the best at the moment, then the risks of low level radiation have been underestimated five to ten times in adults and perhaps 10–15 times in children. This means that low radiation, even that close to background levels, is much more damaging than once thought. As for background radiation itself, those who worked on the Oxford Survey felt it was a major cause of childhood cancers, particularly leukemia. Background radiation is nothing to be shrugged away even if we can do little about some of its components.

Other evidence has come recently from a very thorough reassessment of the Hiroshima and Nagasaki data by the International Commission on Radiological Protection (ICRP). More than four decades later it is known that the two bombs dropped were very similar in their radiation effects, so now all the data from both cities can be pooled to give a much larger "population" for statistical assessment. We also know now that the warm moist air at the time scattered radiation, and the buildings provided considerably more shielding from gamma radiation than we originally thought, so the previous estimates of exposure have been halved. At the same time the carefully kept tumor registries are recording many more lung, liver, cervical, urinary, and prostate cancers, especially in people who were less than ten years old in 1945. People now in their forties and fifties have rates eight times those who were over 35 at the time of the terrible destruction. Even protein damage to red blood cells can still be seen by new blood scanning methods in victims 40 years later.

So convincing was this evidence that Britain's NRPB did not wait for the ICRP to work out its recommendations, but immediately called for a reduction in the annual dose equivalent to less than one-third of the previous level used in atomic industries, and to one-half that used for ordinary people. This means that 50 mSv is reduced to 15 mSv, and the 1 mSv for the public is reduced to 0.5 mSv. "We can't go on waiting," said the director. "We should put people on notice. It would be wrong to wait for two or three years." And although the ICRP tends to act slowly, and has been criticized for doing arithmetic that underestimates the chances of nonfatal cancers, one of its commissioners went on record to suggest "a decrease in dose limits by a factor as high as five."

Every piece of evidence that is coming to light about the effects of low level radiation points to a three- to tenfold reduction in the present "permissible levels," and we must remember that these levels are considered as maximum values not to be exceeded rather than the LARA "low as reasonably achievable" levels recommended by most national authorities. But even as rather conservative national and international bodies of radiation experts are lowering formerly acceptable levels, it comes as no surprise to learn that others are trying to raise them. Immediately after Chernobyl the countries of the Common Market got together and agreed to certain maximum levels in foodstuffs. These were a maximum of 30,000 bq/kg from caesium 137 ingested over the first year, and 5,000 bq/kg per year thereafter. To meet these levels, and making some assumptions about an average European diet (?), they adopted 600 bq/kg as the limit above which food would not be allowed on the market. This was twice the level allowed by Sweden and some other countries, but it served until the end of October 1987, at which time it was due to be reviewed. In April 1987, 49 scientists from the Common Market countries met, with the French and the British initially pushing for a 5,000 bq/kg limit, the Germans and the Dutch recommending the 600 bq limit be kept, and the Danes saying that even this was too high. With the exception of the Germans, there was a direct correlation of the level recommended with the amount each country relied upon atomic power, an association we shall look at again later. Between April and May the scientists cut the levels they considered safe five times, but in November, a month after the original agreement ran out, they still could not come to any decision.

It is difficult to know what is going on in a situation like this, what thinking and preconceptions inform these stances taken and the proposals made. As we have seen, with our rough rule of thumb for caesium 137 that multiplies daily intake of becquerels times days times 1.3×10^{-8} sieverts, even 600 bq day after day means about 2.85 mSv per year, now nearly six times the newly proposed 0.5 mSv level for the general public. Of course, few people are going to ingest a kilogram of food each day for a year at the limit of 600 bq, but a kilogram of food per day is not unreasonable, and even if only a quarter of that kilo contained radioactivity close to the limit, say in the meat, that would still give an annual dose greater than 0.5 mSv recommended because of the almost total retention of the caesium and the relatively long biological halflife of 70 days. And we have not even considered caesium 134, and other components of fallout with shorter halflives, which would increase the absorbed dose. But now we come to the most controversial question of all. What does a millisievert or two, or three, or four ... mean in terms of its effect on people? If we can only estimate probabilities, can we at least predict how many people in a large population, say of a region or country or even Europe as a whole, will contract cancer and die of it as a result of a certain radiation dose? My own, quite personal answer to this, after going carefully through a dozen or more of examples of these sorts of computations, is an absolute and flat *no*. This "no" flies in the face of many "experts," but it is a personally definitive "no" on two grounds. First, because in science it is totally useless at best, and dishonestly misleading at worst, to compute a prediction if it can never be tested to see if it is true or false. And we shall see in a minute that with the possible exception of the Soviet Union's huge epidemiological study, a study that will have to compile data for at least 20 years, we shall never be able to test any prediction made from the most conservative to the wildest – and they come in all varieties to suit every taste.

But my answer is also "no" because all estimates are based on averages so spurious, on assumptions that cover up and distort so much more than they reveal, that no thinking person can even start the arithmetic. And the ground of the spurious nature of all the averages and assumptions is geographical – and geographical on two counts. We simply do not have the information we need on anything approaching a fine enough geographical scale to undertake any computation with confidence. As for our current procedures, they produce so much "spatial averaging" that the results are meaningless. What is "spatial averaging?" It is taking a reindeer herder in Lappland eating foods that may well contain 3,000 bq each day, or 14.2 mSv a year, and adding him to nine farmers in southern Sweden who received negligible fallout, dividing by ten, and then declaring an average of 1.42 mSv. At another geographic scale it is estimating some "average dose" for the whole of Sweden, when the fallout levels go from almost nothing to peaks many thousands of times higher, multiplying by the population in Sweden, ignoring totally that some of the fallout occurred in the sparsely populated north, and then declaring "there is no cause for alarm." Such a computation is not only geographically naive, but it is thoughtless and essentially dishonest because it can only deceive. It is distressing that most scientists are taught to think about *time* – rates are always "per some time units" – but seldom about space. The result is that many of them seldom think through what doing arithmetic over space means for the results and their interpretation. As one thermodynamicist said to me, "It is like putting your head in the freezing compartment of the refrigerator, and your feet on the stove, and telling me you feel nice and warm." Fortunately there are signs that this sort of nonsense is being recognized by scientists other than geographers. Even in the guarded "committee language" of Britain's Radioactive Waste Management Advisory committee, the computation of risks from the collective dose (spatial averaging) concept has been strongly criticized. "The method . . . misleads and is imprecise," the committee concluded, and the numbers "give an impression of precision unwarranted by very imprecise extrapolation. We see the use of a collective dose as being unhelpful in the context of communicating with the public." Yet dozens of such estimates and predictions were made all over Europe after Chernobyl, and you could tell immediately where the person doing the arithmetic was coming from, what the assumptions were, and what preconceptions informed them. Pronuclear proponents grabbed one set of assumptions that went into their arithmetic at one end and produced no cause for alarm at the other. Antinuclear proponents took another set of assumptions and found their arithmetic generated Armageddon. One pronuclear physicist said that Three Mile Island would only produce one cancer death, so by his own assumption Chernobyl, releasing a million times more radioactivity, should produce at least a million cancers. But he would be the first to heap scorn on just such an estimate by an eminent medical physicist who had used the best available geographic and scientific evidence to arrive at this high figure. Most estimates of deaths and malignancies lie between 1,000 and 1 million, a thousandfold range within which the most rabid pro- and anti-nuclear proponents should find what they are looking for. Perhaps it is time to bring some perspective to this very difficult question about which we are so ignorant.

First, can we ever point to a person who has died of cancer and say, "Chernobyl caused it?" Generally the answer is "no," unless we find someone so contaminated with caesium in muscles or kidney that we cannot put commonsense aside. But in general the answer is "no" because we can only try to estimate excess deaths in a large population for which cancer may already be a leading cause of death. One study focusing on Britain estimated 40 extra deaths over the next 50 years when 200,000 people in Britain die of cancer each year. Another estimated 1,000 extra deaths in European Common Market countries over 50 years when 30 million might be expected to die of cancer in this time anyway. And given increasing chemical pollution of air and groundwater in many parts of Europe, could we even find a million extra deaths out of 30 million and say definitively that they were due to Chernobyl rather than chemicals like PCBs or heavy metal pollution from cadmium, lead, mercury, and so on? The answer is almost certainly no, and no for two reasons. First, Europe is not even collecting and collating the data that might be used 30 or 40 years from now to find these effects. Secondly, so many other things mask the effects of radiation that we may never be able to make any definitive statement. We have arrived at a very general problem in scientific inquiry, the problem of finding the "signal in the noise." The phrase comes straight out of electronics: if you have a very faint signal which is a pure undistorted wave, you can always subject it to so much random noise that it is completely masked and obliterated. This of course is the principle of jamming radio broadcasts you do not want people to hear. But filtering electronic signals to clean them up is a relatively simple matter compared to filtering the noise of other cancer deaths away to reveal the Chernobyl effect. I do not think there is anyone who claims to be able to do it.

So if no one can find the signal anyway, does that mean that we do not have to worry? The answer is obviously not: somewhere between the 1,000 and 1 million excess deaths for Europe lies the true figure presumable known only to . . . whoever or whatever you want to call it, her or him. The exact number is certainly beyond mortal arithmetic. The problem is that doing such arithmetic tends to act as a sort of scientific soporific, it numbs thinking about the things that the arithmetic is about. Except, of course, they are not things but people, and notice how easily our thinking slips into this "thingified" mode, this reified approach, and how the language that we use to talk about it betrays us. Those numbers somewhere between a thousand and a million are not things but my husband, my child, my father, my lover. The "excess cancers" are you and me. Except that it will always happen to someone else. So why worry?

But many do worry. Some translate their worry into action, into decisions about what they buy and eat, into decisions to work or to contribute in some way towards a world in which the chances of Chernobyl are lessened. Others rely on "them" to make the decisions, because "they" know what is safe and what is not. Surely "they" – the government officials, nuclear scientists, atomic experts – surely "they" know what they are doing and would not act irresponsibly? Surely "they," trained in science and the search for truth, elected to high office and holding the trust of the people, surely "they" will not let us down?

So let us return from this scientific and technical excursion to the concrete reality of those first days and weeks after Chernobyl and see what "they" said and did – and did not.

10 Eastern Europe: Now I know the official explanation I'm still frightened

The information that there was a reactor accident at Chernobyl produced its own information crisis. All over Europe switchboards jammed as people tried to get reliable information and advice. No one had made preparations for such a telephonic onslaught, perhaps because even those charged with the responsibility of dealing with these events never really believed they could happen. To prepare for atomic disaster you have to believe it is a real and distinct possibility and that something can be done about it. Otherwise planning for the impossible becomes a charade, a going-through-the-bureaucratic-motions with the motions themselves uninformed by a lively and prescient imagination of what an actual scenario could look like.

No one was prepared. Even those countries with atomic power and some sort of "National Radiation Board" in place were unable to cope. Some had derisory plans to handle small evacuations around their own national facilities. Few had even thought about a danger blowing across their borders. Some countries had nothing in place to measure, collate, assess, and interpret the data, let alone the facilities to advise the media and the public about their meaning and implications.

Nor, apparently, did they have enough knowledge to advise anyway. The first switchboards to be jammed were those of the World Health Organization's regional office at Copenhagen, as national government agencies asked "What shall we do?" in order to answer the same question back home. The early days of the crisis were marked by national bureaucratic incompetence, muddle and outright dissimulation never quite seen before on such a widespread international scale. No one seemed to be able to explain anything, and what information and advice were given nearly always conflicted with what someone else had said before.

Even the United Nation's agencies, the World Health Organization (WHO) at Geneva and Copenhagen, and the International Atomic

Energy Agency (IAEA) at Vienna were ill prepared for the flood of requests for help by national governments, although they responded promptly to the new tasks that had been suddenly dumped upon them. All acknowledge that the IAEA played an important role as a collecting and clearing house for large and diverse amounts of information. On May 6, the day after the fire was put out, 18 experts in radiation medicine and technology were brought together in Copenhagen by WHO to pool their knowledge and give advice. They did the best they could, but by this time the worst of the fallout was over and little more than reassurances could be given, laced with a few cautions about hot spots, local concentrations of iodine 131 in the milk, and the importance of washing vegetables.

But if you happen to be in a hot spot what do you do? As for precautions about iodine 131 in milk, they were "old hat" by this time. Anyway, who had a household scintillometer in the kitchen? As for vegetables, we shall see that some of this advice was misplaced because the experts themselves had little experience and few hard facts on which to base their judgements. But in a crisis you do the best you can, and perhaps those who were called to Copenhagen knew better than most how little they knew. A major recommendation of their report asked for an international system to be established so that any similar crisis in the future could be monitored on more than a piecemeal national and local basis. Nevertheless, if a reactor loaded with plutonium 239 blows up in France tomorrow the switchboards will jam again, because the issue has been defused in the traditional bureaucratic way by setting up committees, and three years later the committees were still studying the problem.

A lack of information, conflicting information, an inability to know what to do with information – little wonder that there was such widespread anxiety. In those first ten days no useful news came from the Soviet Union, and what was known had to be pieced together from widely scattered sources in a variety of different languages using half-a-dozen different units of measurement. With meagre facts making up a tattered and threadbare scientific "text" it was hardly surprising that interpretations should differ and lead to conflicting reports. And what do you do anyway? Unless you are trained in these highly specialized areas of radiation physics and health care there is not much you can do except sit there numbly wondering if the children are going to be alright. As for those smooth assurances and glib statements that there was "no cause for alarm," these came from the people who originally brought you "it can never happen anyway." Another thing that blew up in those early days was public trust.

And now we have to think like geographers – bringing space and time together as an event of the physical world impinges upon the human. In our mind's eye we have to hover above Europe in our earth satellite and create a mental picture of a dynamic map. As the radioactive cloud physically swirled and dispersed around Europe it left behind similar swirls and eddies in the human condition. If you were down on the ground it was difficult to stand apart and watch it like a detached spectator at a show. As it came closer to home you became more involved and part of the confusion. An explosion at Chernobyl? Jaså ... Well, it's far away ... Tough on the poor Russians, but after all it's their reactor. Bad fallout over Sweden? Das ist ja schade, bei uns it's a beautiful spring day at Kitzbuhl in Austria. Radioactive iodine in Austria? Poor beggars, but at least we don't have to cope with that here in Liverpool. Radioactive iodine in Liverpool's milk? How frightfully lucky we live in Kent ... Different people reacted in different ways according to what they knew, and, just as important sometimes, according to what they did not know. Some even took their own lives, knowingly to end them, and unknowingly from homemade iodine doses, but all thinking that they were doing the right thing.

In Poland the radioactivity was monitored closely as the 140 stations went on alert and reported every 2 hours to Warsaw. Poland, along with all the Eastern bloc countries, had an international treaty in force with the Soviet Union that in the event of any atomic accident the one involved would immediately inform the others. But now there was only silence. A Soviet nuclear planner interviewed a month later said "The Polish government was informed very quickly via direct channels," but this was totally false and denied by the Poles themselves. The rains started falling in eastern Poland, and at Mikolajki the radioactivity of the air soared from 700 to 15,000 times the background levels. Wherever the rains fell they left their "footprints," wet spots on the earth's surface that could be detected for days afterwards from satellites measuring infrared radiation. But rainspots became hot spots, some only tens of meters wide, others several kilometers in diameter. No one except the Polish authorities knows exactly where these are. One government spokesman said bluntly at a television interview "It is not good to give people unnecessary facts ... ordinary people cannot draw conclusions." Even those long suspicious of government arrogance and coverups never thought they would hear someone say so blatantly in public what many knew from bitter experience. Very little appeared in either the local or regional press, and a sociologist's analysis of newspaper reporting remains unpublished to this day.

But in a moment of crisis Poland's size, and the nature of her highly centralized government, paid off in decision and action. Given the facts as they were coming in during those first few days, with radiation levels mounting across the country, and with upper air levels checked constantly by Polish airforce planes, the Poles acted. On April 29 children and adults in the hard hit Bialystok region began to receive doses of "Lugol," the ordinary iodine in liquid form, and at the same time ambulances supplied the mixture to the "nomenklatura," the high up members of the party bureaucracy. The next day the same doses were available across the country for less privileged people. It was an extraordinary mass exercise in public health, fully justified by the facts and circumstances as they were known at the time, and an experiment carefully monitored ever since. No adverse effects have been reported, and the stable iodine clearly reduced the radioactive intake. In some cases in northeastern Poland the iodine 131 had already entered the food chain and a few children were found to have extremely high levels in their thyroid glands. One poor lad had 370 mSv, but he was one of the exceptions. It was a courageous decision of the Polish authorities to act, and a remarkable national effort in which the more than 3,000 pharmacies distributed the brown solution to 18 million people through schools, nurseries, hospitals, and places of work.

Milk was the first food to be carefully monitored, and powdered milk was substituted for weeks, especially for children, who are particularly vunerable with their small thyroids and still so much growing up to do. Fresh uncontaminated milk was also donated and flown to Poland from as far away as Britain. Vegetables from the eastern and northeastern parts of Poland were registering up to 253,000 bq/kg and were condemned. Grass registered 150,000 bq, and all grazing animals were required to remain inside their barns to feed on pre-Chernobyl fodder. All foods registering more than 5,000 bq were prohibited for sale, a level roughly 17 times as high as that adopted in Sweden and West Germany, but when you are poor and already have food problems what else can you do?

And then the story from Poland stopped. Up to December 1986 reports from Poland were remarkably open and frank as she tried to contribute her knowledge about the human and the environmental impact to the larger world community. Her own scientists acknowledged in turn the pivotal help given to them by the IAEA in Vienna. With fallout effects scattered over 20 million square kilometers of Europe you need to piece together every bit of information you can get and slot it into its geographic location. That is how science works, piecing together evidence openly and for the common good. But someone, somewhere, slammed the gate shut. Since the end of 1986 it has been almost impossible to get hard information. One Polish scholar managed to get a letter out saying he had been expressly forbidden to show any interest in the problem, and although there are some official reports and studies they are circulated within a very small group. "Is rather detective work" he wrote, and as we shall see much of the story everywhere is a matter of fitting many small pieces of the puzzle together. Even Poles living abroad were hesitant to say or report anything for fear of jeopardizing friends or relatives, and Sweden expelled one Polish vice-consul for spying on his own countrymen in exile.

But in the absence of facts rumors abound and only serve to keep anxiety high. Though they may not have the status of acceptable scientific evidence they cannot be ignored by anyone genuinely concerned for the human, as opposed to the simple physical condition. The few direct communications we have from letters and visits all attest to widespread anxiety, the "Chernobyl neurosis" as one person described it, not the least in Gdansk close to Zarnowiec where the first Polish atomic energy plant is being built. In the Carpathian mountains of southern Poland there were early reports of widespread kills of bees, as the new spring flowers opened their petals to the sun, and also to the iodine, caesium, and other radionuclides, forcing the bees to gather packets of radioactive pollen to feed their larvae. But the hives of the region had also experienced a deadly disease for several years before, and it is impossible to know whether the bee kills were due to this or the fallout. Isolating a true Chernobyl effect is very difficult. As for direct medical effects on people, official reports denied that there was any damage at all. But a pediatrician in northeastern Poland said that congenital effects had been observed, and that thyroid readings in some of the children from the hot spots were extremely high. We know from the children of Rongelap, a small island in the South Pacific smothered in fallout from atomic bomb tests, that early death and stunted growth result from such overexposure.

As one might expect in a country that has somehow maintained its national identity and language over hundreds of years of invasion, annexation, and war, many of the true feelings came out in bitter jokes. "At first I was frightened," said one woman at the hairdresser, "but now that I have heard all the explanations I am still frightened." "Well," said her friend, "has anything good for Poland ever come on a wind from the east?" As for the iodine solution for saturating the thyroid, the Poles called it "Russian Coca-Cola." But underneath the jokes there was desperate concern. In Bialystok, 3,000 people had the courage to sign their names to a petition to halt the building of the Zarnowiec reactors, and the best-known clandestine paper of Solidarity, *Tygodnik Mazowsze*, blasted the Soviets for failing to provide information until much of the damage had been done.

Elsewhere in eastern Europe the story is the same – a clampdown on news and discussion even under the prodding of a *glasnost* policy from the east. Czechoslovakia, East Germany, Hungary, and Bulgaria already have 16 Soviet designed reactors in operation, and Romania is building three more not far from Bucharest. With plans to increase nuclear power by 500 percent by the year 2000, fallout from an exploding Soviet reactor is an embarrassment that governments hope will go away. The Czech government, one week after the fire was put out, said the fallout had completely avoided Czech territory, but radiation measurements made on bottled mushrooms a year later were so high that the mushrooms had to be discarded. Unfortunately, these and other figures were never published by the Czech government for its own people. In Romania vegetables reached 8,813 bq/kg and were withdrawn from the market, and so was sheep's milk at 6,290 bq/litre. Both Romania and Bulgaria were hampered in their monitoring efforts by a lack of modern, sensitive equipment, and called upon outside aid to help them with their predicaments.

Many Eastern bloc countries rely heavily on agricultural exports to the West for hard currencies, but few of the traditional agricultural exports from eastern Europe passed the scintillometers at the borders, and the Soviet Union bought up large quantities that had been banned by western Europe. This produced a hard currency crisis, with Romania suspending $300 million in loan repayments to Austrian banks. Poland lost $40–60 million in food exports, as well as over $6 million in domestic foods. Lettuces, for example, plummeted from 300 to 3 zlotys on the Warsaw market.

But "no news" about environmental pollution in eastern Europe is nothing new. Much of southern Poland and eastern Czechoslovakia is a cesspit created by widespread chemical pollution that produces a high proportion of the acid rain all over Europe and highly contaminated water supplies locally. Many groundwater aquifers contain appalling levels of chemicals and heavy metals, and huge slagheaps lie only 500 meters from principal urban water reservoirs. In Silesia heavy metals in water are often 50 times above internationally accepted maximum levels, and half of Poland's rivers do not meet even minimal standards. Some prominent environmentalists in Sweden have even suggested that the cheapest and most effective way to get rid of acid rain from eastern Europe is to offer the Czechs and others modern gas scrubbing plants as gifts. But even these would leave large areas laced with chemicals in the ground and water, chemicals that appear highly resistant to natural processes of biodegration. Nor is publicity, let alone opposition easy. In Czechoslovakia over 100 scientists, many of whom belong to the Slovak Academy of Sciences, produced an impeccable report on the chronic and wholesale chemical pollution of Bratislava. They were rounded up by the security police, interrogated, and then threatened unless they repudiated their report.

So piecing together the full impact on eastern Europe is not easy. Our only hope is that one day the true and full story will come out so that we can all learn from this unexpected and bitter experiment. The facts from this part of Europe are particularly important because it is so close to Chernobyl and received a relatively higher fallout of larger particles. But what about western Europe, where most of the mass media is free to report, and "democratic" governments are meant to be highly responsive and responsible to the people? Unfortunately, bureaucracies tend to be the same dissimulating organizations everywhere. After all, most people are ignorant and not to be trusted with "matters of state."

11 Western Europe: So why did you say something else yesterday?

Outside of Scandinavia the first countries of western Europe to feel the effects of Chernobyl were those sharing the great alpine chain from Austria through Switzerland and Italy to France. Highly aware of the air pollution coming from its northeastern neighbors, and concerned about the water quality of the Danube flowing through much of the country, Austria already had a strong environmental lobby, and many within the various political parties took environmental issues seriously. Vienna is also the headquarters of the International Atomic Energy Agency (IAEA), so in those early days Austria became a focus for heavy flows of information from all over Europe. She was also able to monitor the fallout at a finer geographic scale than any other country in the world, and so built up an almost movie-like sequence of maps hour by hour to put her people on the alert. Austria also made use of the precise analytical capabilities of the IAEA laboratory itself. Careful work there showed the presence of 19 different radionuclides in the fallout immediately around Vienna, registering up to 102,000 bq in a square meter of grass by May 3. Fortunately most of these decayed rapidly, and a month later the levels had fallen to about 1,500 bq with larger hot particles giving readings many times higher.

Readings from low lying areas may be deceptively low, and in her mountains Austria paid a high price both in anxiety and hard cash. Nearly the entire strawberry crop was discarded, and $80 million was eventually paid to her farmers for losses. Even today great uncertainty exists about foods from the higher alpine pastures. By the first autumn (1986) the caesium 134 and 137 in Styria and similar alpine regions raised radiation levels in redcurrants and blueberries to above 1,000 bq, and radioactive ruthenium 103 added another 200. Playing safe, Austria adopted one of the lowest permissible levels in Europe for human foodstuffs (111 bq/kg), and 80 percent of the berry crops exceeded this. One government source said that most of the berries would probably be below the limit after washing, but later evidence contradicted this as we shall see. Much of the radioactivity by the autumn was systemic, meaning that the plants had taken up the caesium from the soil. It was no longer lying on the surface of the fruit, most of which had not even flowered and formed in the high alp by late April.

The Alps, with their high rainfall, were really a major problem, and those of northern Italy were hit hard, producing the highest levels of radioactivity in the milk of any western European country, 12 times the levels at which the US Food and Drug Administration requires milk to be removed from sale. By May 3 leafy vegetables were up to 7,610 bq, and three days later levels rose to the thousands in central and southern Italy. And at a time when bureaucratic bungling was already apparent, Italy's ministries exceeded even the most cynical predictions. The Ministry for Civil Protection first announced that radiation levels were so low that there was "no cause for alarm," a government phrase in many European languages that now signals that something is seriously wrong. Accompanied by a coy suggestion that you might want to rinse your lettuce, what this official announcement was based on no one has ever been able to determine. It was contradicted quickly by the Ministry of Health, which quite properly banned consumption of contaminated milk by pregnant women and all children under 10 years old. These contradictory government announcements, together with other confusing statements by ministers and "spokesmen" who claimed both the responsibility and the publicity that came with it, created a genuine panic in many parts of Italy. Pharmacies and supermarkets had their shelves stripped of canned and frozen foods, soft drinks and mineral water, powdered and long-lasting milk, and, distressingly, iodine in all forms, from pure crystals to the tinctures put on cuts and grazes. Few had the faintest idea of the doses involved, doses that were quite unnecessary anyway, and some died from chronic and self-administered potions.

Having produced panic, dissimulation was then tried to calm things down. High radiation measures from the Alps were averaged by government scientists with low readings from the south to give innocuous "regional values," which gave as usual "no cause for alarm." We know this arithmetic is what a geographer calls "spatial averaging" and we have seen how false it can be. People, and perhaps especially Italian mothers concerned for the safety of their children, are not fools. When levels in northern Italy are declared to be "no cause for alarm," and a few kilometers across the border in Switzerland the TV announcer is telling the unaveraged and unvarnished truth that levels are 100 times higher, even people without technical training can do their own arithmetic. At this time laboratories independent of the nuclear power industry had established levels in the soil as high as 79,300 bq/m^2 in the Ispra Alps. Little wonder that half the Italians in a poll conducted at the time said they did not believe their own government's figures.

Nor did it help matters when Italy's atomic energy commission refused to release information about caesium and strontium in food, and some of its scientists anonymously told reporters of the *International Courier* to contact university scientists because "They are not restrained the way we are." When pressed again about withholding caesium figures, one spokesman of the Civil Protection Agency simply said "What do you want with those figures? By now the damage is done. Whatever caesium there is has been absorbed into our bodies. We'll see the long-term effects only after many years." When vegetables from the north were sold with contamination levels more than 60 percent above those allowed by Italian law, the Atomic Energy Commission and the Civil Protection Agency answered by referring reporters to each other.

Even international reports were interdicted. When WHO published its first and totally public report from Copenhagen on the effects of the fallout on Europe the Italian government classified the report as "Confidential" and refused to release it, saying it was being held up for a few days "for minor typographical corrections." It was then learnt that milk high in iodine 131 had appeared in cartons date-stamped before Chernobyl, and that milk supposedly thrown away had been secretly kept for long-life milk and yogurt. The following October independent scientists at the University of Milan found powdered milk in a number of baby formulas to be "so significantly contaminated by caesium that it required urgent intervention by health authorities." No wonder the Italian people had so little confidence in the face of all the lying by its own government.

Across the Adriatic in Greece there was also confusion made worse by intense political rivalries. As a portion of the radioactive airmass moved south it deposited fallout on fields already ripening with durum winter wheat just before the harvest period. Much of the wheat had to be condemned, but simply disposing of it became a problem. Some thought it could be ground up and dumped back on the fields in the hope that the caesium would bind to clay particles, but with the caesium radionuclides having halflives of 2.4 and 28 years few were sure that this would solve anything. We now know, from subsequent studies in Europe, that these doubts were fully justified. As for the government, it gave no information to the people until May 6, and then in so many unfamiliar units that no one understood anything. As a result there was some panic, accompanied by demonstrations against nuclear power, and a group of doctors, lawyers, and scientists formed an independent organization to test foods. Delaying information makes trust evaporate even faster, unless you have a high degree of control over most forms of public communication, and Greece had some of the heaviest fallout in all of western Europe from the last days of the Chernobyl plume. In Turkey, for example, the whole question of food contamination was played down by the government, although the large tea crop in the north was badly contaminated as the radioactive cloud moved across the Black Sea from Chernobyl and hit the high slopes of the tea-growing areas. But to replace the large quantities of tea that the Turks consume each year with imports would have cost a fortune in hard foreign currency. So little was done, and perhaps the consequences will never be known. Certainly nothing is being monitored or recorded that would allow a scientific assessment to be made.

Further north, in Switzerland and West Germany, the story was a little different. Information and advice came from many sources, although much of it was conflicting. In general the Swiss government acted cautiously, when it acted at all, but in that multilingual country television broadcasts are picked up from all the neighbors. Italian TV said there was a ban on northern milk, German TV said there was no ban on milk, and French TV said nothing at all. Perhaps the most reliable information came from just over Switzerland's border, from the West German town of Konstanz, where the university's physicists detected the cloud on April 30 after heavy rains and immediately started monitoring the fallout and conducting a series of experiments. On the ground the radiation levels rose rapidly to 194,000 bq/m², about two-thirds of the highest levels reported from Munich 150 kilometers away at 315,000 bq, while water registered about 125,000 bq/litre. These values were 15–20 times higher than those recorded in Stuttgart only 120 kilometers away, confirming the highly spotty nature of fallout patterns. Officials in Stuttgart, the capital of Baden in which Konstanz lies, said there was no cause for alarm, because Stuttgart itself was considered safe, a nice example of the "I'm-in-the-boat-Jack-shove-off" syndrome. Feeling secure themselves they did not order cows to be removed from the fields, did not restrict milk consumption, but advised people to wash vegetables "just in case," all on the grounds of correct and proper uniformity of official central directives when the fallout was anything but properly uniform.

The measurements and experiments made by the Konstanz physicists provided very precise hard data, including some facts that nobody had bothered to establish before. Apparently in the entire scientific literature there was nothing on the effects of washing vegetables contaminated by radioactive fallout. When this simple "experiment" was actually made, with careful measurements before and after, it turned out that only about 10 percent of the radioactivity was removed. This was confirmed later by the Austrians, and it meant that all the advice about washing spinach and berries was simply wrong. The Konstanz scientists also tested contaminated grass and showed that even when rapidly dried and shaken it retained

90 percent of the radiation, so carrying the danger into the future when the grass would be used as fodder. Moreover, dried hay is dusty stuff, so those moving it around, either from one place to another, or simply throwing bundles from hay lofts down into cow stalls, would inhale many small radioactive particles. We shall see that these can cause great damage to lung tissue.

Nor could the physicists find much in the literature about soil contamination, so they marked off a square meter on the ground, peeled off 1 centimeter at a time, and carefully measured the radioactive content of each layer. It turned out that most of the contamination was in the first 8–10 centimeters, a figure confirmed by the Swedes and justifying the measures in the Soviet Union of scraping off the first 10 centimeters of soil around Chernobyl for concentrated burial. Finally, after ten days of intense scientific activity, even Stuttgart could no longer deny the meticulous data and rather pompously designated Konstanz as an official monitoring station. But the people of Konstanz had already taken the advice of their local scientists. It was just as well that they did: 3 litres of the local milk would have taken an adult up to the annual permissible limit, and less than a kilogram of leafy vegetables would have done the same. Children were even more at risk and were warned not to play in dusty playgrounds and sandboxes to prevent them from inhaling radioactive particles. Unfortunately, just across the border in the Canton of Thurgau in Switzerland, no warnings had been given by either the local or central governments and the people were exposed quite unnecessarily to the dangers.

In many ways West Germany is a remarkable country, with a federal structure giving a high degree of local control to the states. These "states rights" are jealously guarded, with the result that reactions to the radioactive contamination varied widely, with different limits adopted, and different sorts of information provided. Germany is already 30 percent dependent on atomic power, with 20 reactors now in operation, so the Establishment at the Federal level tends to be strongly pronuclear, playing down anything that might raise doubts or strengthen the antinuclear movement. Generally the official announcements were soothing, even as sheep's milk hit 5,500 bq and spinach 2,500. On April 30 WHO reported 315,000 bq/m^2 on the ground at Munich, and it is now acknowledged the restrictions on food were issued too late.

At the state level reactions also varied. Those with fairly conservative governments followed the Federal lead by playing the dangers down, while those with Social Democratic governments and higher proportions of the Green Party tried to warn their people much more responsibly. Hess and Saar, for example, gave highly reliable information as it appeared from tests and monitoring, and the Greens even published reports in a number of languages for foreigners working in, or simply visiting, Germany. Over a year later, weekly reports were available announcing results of more than 100 analyses of different food products, and maps were compiled and published by independent groups to show where high levels of caesium were still a problem.

But if attitudes and information vary widely within a country like West Germany, the variation pales beside that found on either side of international borders. Nowhere is this contrast seen more vividly than between Germany and France, particularly between the open, informative and concerned Saar, and the truculent department of Lorraine with the nuclear power plant at Cattenom only a few kilometers inside France. "There is a kind of information blockage at the border," said the Minister of the Environment for Saar, where very careful precautions were taken during the height of the fallout. This was at a time when vegetables in nearby Alsace were registering 35,000 bq with iodine 131, and still 7,000 bq a year later from caesium contamination systemically absorbed. But France blandly ignored these figures. Even on May 6, eight days after the cloud arrived, the French Minister for Agriculture said that because of its location France had been totally spared any radioactive fallout, while the government channels of French television showed weather maps with "STOP" signs all along the eastern border. Four days later spinach from Alsace was taken off the market, only to be frozen for future use. "Imagine a field divided between France and Germany," said the Saar's minister, "At the French end everything was normal. Children were playing and cattle were grazing. At the German end there were no children and no cattle. I saw such things with my own eyes."

France's dependence on atomic power is higher than any other country in the world, with 65 percent of its electrical energy coming from reactors, and still going up. No matter what government party is in power, the interlocked elite of French society allows nothing to rock the atomic boat and any disturbing news is heavily suppressed. "There has long been a consensus among the elite that France has no choice but nuclear deterrence and nuclear energy," said one of the directors of the French Institute of International Relations, "So anything that threatens to shake public confidence in either is covered up." But even France has pores in its thick shell and information from the outside world slowly oozes through. After a few days several newspapers denounced the government for blatant lying, and slowly, weeks later, the extraordinary coverup of those early days came out. Reacting to the bitter controversy and charges, the Minister of Industry admitted that "information had been passed on badly," but the newspapers charged that the truth had been deliberately withheld out of fear of the nuclear power industry and the effects on agricultural prices and sales. When the director of the Radiation Protection Service was asked why information had not been given to the public, he said "Simply because there were two holidays in two weeks, and it was very complicated to transmit the data." He also insisted that his service had issued 200 informative bulletins, but Agence France-Presse said that it had received only 12 – all of which had been published.

In light of these charges the government appointed a committee "to shed all possible light on the consequences to France," fully staffed with experts from the nuclear power industry. But as the leader of France's tiny Green Party pointed out "We already have two government commissions to monitor nuclear safety. What we need is an independent commission of nongovernment experts with access to reliable information."

The French Commission on Atomic Energy has been called a "state within a state," and can do just about anything it likes. Virtually all information is highly controlled by agencies directly connected to the nuclear power industry, and as three French scientists noted "The public is kept in infantile ignorance." Generating sound information independently is difficult, but by patient work, and not a few rather helpful "unofficial transmissions of official data," a large and highly respected national consumer group was able to piece together an overall picture and publish it as a special issue of *Que Choisir?* (What to choose?) on the first anniversary of the accident. An independent laboratory used by the consumer group first established with French data a very high correlation between rainfall and fallout, so that one became a good surrogate measure for the other. For example, in southeastern France, Cadarache had 10 millimeters of rain and 14,000 bq/m^2 on the ground, Marcoule had 30 millimeters and 42,500 while 50 kilometers to the north Cruas had well over 30 millimeters and 252,000. A rainfall map from April 30 to May 6, carefully compiled from 3,500 daily readings all over France, was the first information available to the French showing where the danger had been, and perhaps still was. Curiously, when the French Electricity Board and the Atomic Energy Commission (whose scientists had made the original measurements) transmitted the figures to the Radiation Protection Board, the 252,000 bq at Cruas had somehow become 42,000 while the 42,500 at Morcoule had "spontaneously decayed" to 11,600. Even the laws of physics can be set aside by a bureaucratic elite. The consumer group also charged that other results had been systematically lowered by the Ministry of Health. Even a year later some vegetables tested in the northeast had 7,000 bq, and winter feed for cattle in the *département* of the Drome was registering 5,000–6,000. Goat's cheese was also contaminated, for goats range widely over high pastures where rainfall and radioactivity are high.

And so the cloud moved on: through Belgium, where a daily bulletin provided little information in a country heavily dependent (60 percent) on nuclear energy, and through Holland where bulletins were first directed to producers of foodstuffs, leaving most of the people in the country in a highly anxious state and wondering why the facts were not being given to them. In fact, both countries escaped very lightly as the air mass crossed the channel without rain scavenging the fallout. Only when it hit the high hills of Wales, Cumbria and the Scottish Highlands did the rain pull the radioactivity down, twice in five days as the air mass corkscrewed out over the Atlantic and then came back to hit Wales and Cumbria a second time.

In Britain the arrival of the cloud caused the now usual and all too familiar reaction. No one was prepared, despite two days of prior warning from Sweden, and an early warning from routine monitoring at Charing Cross Hospital in London. This was despite the fact that Britain was the only western European country to have had experience of a nuclear accident involving a graphite fire. Even this was unable to engender much thought in Whitehalls' phlegmatic imagination because civil servants had been assured by their scientists that a major radioactive release could not possibly occur. British scientists and public relations specialists had attended the Three Mile Island hearings in the United States, but evacuation plans for a major atomic plant still consisted of 23 policeman walking around without any protective clothing to advise the local inhabitants to go to an evacuation center two miles away, and otherwise to do what they could "to promote mutual assistance among the public."

The result was that the telephone exchange at the National Radiation Protection Board (NRPB) locked solid when it opened at eight o'clock in the morning, and it remained jammed for days. Even official inquiries received a constant busy signal. Days later a second 'hot line' was opened by the Ministry of the Environment, only to be immediately jammed by calls from people trying to get reliable information. In the meantime the Secretary of State for the Environment assured the House of Commons that there was no cause for alarm, while newspapers described the situation as "little short of a shambles," with "Government public relations officials, with little or no knowledge of the subject, feeding incomprehensible statistics to equally baffled journalists in the name of defusing public alarm." The Friends of the Earth said the government's attitude "drifted between the patronizing, complacent and downright incompetent," while others blasted the official world for an "underreaction."

The real tragedy of mismanagement was that every local authority in Britain has environmental health officers (EHOs) and an excellent network used by the National Food Hazard Warning System to notify people in case dangerous or contaminated foodstuffs have to be taken off the market. No use was made of this ready made information network, and the EHOs themselves said that they could not trust the government's often contradictory statements and that they required an independent source of information. Trust in government statements was not enhanced when radioactivity levels in food and milk approached, and in some cases exceeded, a set of newly recommended safety limits by the NRPB. These were still three and four times higher than those adopted by Germany and the United States, but as soon as measurements from Scotland showed that even these newly recommended limits might be exceeded, the government backpedalled vigorously and said they were not official, legal, and with statutory force yet. Therefore there was no cause for alarm. A year later a "special Whitehall committee," staffed by Whitehall civil servants, was set up to examine the claims that the whole thing had been mismanaged by Whitehall. One scientific editorial noted that any system recommended by the committee to deal with future incidents "will have to be proof against ministerial inclinations to dissemble and to be 'economical with the truth'."

The truth only came out gradually, with some controversy between scientific bodies about the intensity and geographical extent of fallout. The high fallout area on one official map stopped just a pencil line short of Glasgow, although the rainfall measured at Govan near the city center had the highest radioactivity anywhere in Britain. In the countryside the iodine 131 immediately started to move through the food chain, and children in Dumfries were drinking milk at levels that quickly brought their small thyroids to the annual permissible level. Even the NRPB, employing the meaningless geographic average "over the North," indicated that babies would get to this annual level through ingesting milk and foodstuffs, although much of it could have been avoided. At this point, May 14, NRPB plans to test radioactivity levels in children's thyroids in Glasgow were abandoned "because parents would be alarmed." This, together with discrepancies between ministerial pronouncements and scientific reports did nothing to allay fears.

Iodine decays quickly, however, and the problems that Britain faces today are the long-term effects of the two caesiums, 134 and 137. The problems remain particularly acute in the high pastures of Wales,

Cumbria and Scotland where more than 4 million sheep were restricted for sale or slaughter. One million or more were still affected and banned from the market two years later. The ban started with the usual official dissimulation because the government should have acted on May 14, when caesium levels in Cumbrian sheep rose to 2,450 bq/kg, well over the 1,000 limit. This was when the Minister for Agriculture was saying "We have always been a long way from the stage when we might need to contemplate imposing any sort of restriction." Five weeks later one sheep farmer near Sellafield was told that no one was in any danger, and was actually rebuked by officials for raising such a question. A few days later, on June 20, he received notice that he was forbidden to move any of his sheep, even to lower pastures much less contaminated, although he noted "our products won't be foodstuffs until next year. Why ban their movement? Some won't be food for two years." The area around Sellafield is a particularly touchy one for the government, and when high levels of caesium were found in the pastures around the atomic reprocessing plant the government claimed that it was due to Chernobyl fallout. Unfortunately, meticulous research by the Institute of Terrestrial Ecology on the effects of Sellafield discharges into the Irish Sea, and smokestack discharges into the air, showed that sheep feeding on the surrounding saltmarsh had been taking in 5,000 bq in their winter feed two years before Chernobyl.

A year after the cloud passed over, compensation payments to farmers in Britain were nearly $10 million and still going up. Most of the initial estimates for the decline in caesium uptake by the sheep had proved quite wrong, and some areas that had been taken off the restricted list had been put back on. The mathematical models predicting the rate at which caesium would be removed from the environment had all been calibrated on lowland areas of England with a very high clay content in their soils. At the molecular level clays and micas are arranged in a series of layers with a lattice-like structure, and the caesium ions gradually migrate into these tiny gaps where they are locked in and made much less available as nutrients for plants. But the upland soils of Wales, Cumbria, and Scotland are formed from old Cambrian rocks, and they are acid, low in clay and high in organic matter. There is not much in them to lock the caesium up, and there is some evidence that the acids in the soils actually make metals more available to plants. The result is that grasses and fodder plants take up the radionuclides systemically and are then grazed by the sheep. Sheep also crop very low to the ground and may ingest soil with their feed. In the first few months readings of over 15,000 bq/m^2 were made on Cumbrian pastures, producing 4,130 bq/kg of dry feed, and even a year later fodders had up to 3,391 bq. Most sheep on upland grazing were showing levels of well over 1,000 bq/kg, the legal limit for food adopted by the Euratom Treaty of May 1986.

It is difficult to know what to do with thousands of square kilometers of upland pasture contaminated in this way. The contamination is very spotty on a gross geographic scale, reflecting the pattern of rainfall that brought it down, but it can be even more variable at the scale of a single pasture. There is strong evidence that the wetter areas of a field are more highly contaminated, presumably because caesium is slowly washed into them, and the sheep themselves may form even more concentrated patches. Like many grazing animals they range widely and actually form good "spatial samplers" of the radioactivity in an environment. Then, when herded together, their droppings and urine remove some of the caesium from their muscles at the rate of a biological halflife (time in the sheep) of about ten days, so concentrating the caesium 137 with a physical halflife of 28 years. Two years later even worse news was to come, and it was totally unexpected. Not only did the acid soil conditions make the caesium more readily available to plants, but it also made it transfer through the gut wall of sheep four to ten times more readily than in the first few months after Chernobyl. A great deal of scientific work is being carried out on caesium decline, but neither scientists nor officials are able to commit themselves to a date when once again "sheep may safely graze."

Even two years later a European shipment of 600 tons of meat to Venezuela was turned back to Rotterdam, the port of shipment, because it exceeded international and Common Market levels of radiation. Dutch dock workers refused to unload it, and one proposal was to leach the radionuclides out with acid and dispose of the concentrated radioactivity "safely" – at a cost of $30/kg, or $16 million for the entire shipment.

Sometimes the feelings of impotence and anger at so much official lying, dissimulation and incompetence can only be released in wry humor. One person confused by the millirads, picocuries, microröntgens and becquerels suggested that we needed a measure that was immediately intelligible to ordinary people. This was the "concern," divided into various grades for labelling nuclear "incidents" – the now-common euphemism used to take the distressingly sharp edge of truth off the word "accident." For example:

A microconcern	someone at the Sellafield nuclear reprocessing plant forgot to lock up his overalls.
A miniconcern	children may drink tap water but must not jump in puddles.
A concern	enough luminous sheep in the district to threaten a marginal seat in an election.

A kiloconcern   a disaster the government said wasn't one, e.g. Three
                   Mile Island.

A megaconcern   a disaster that everyone knows was one, whatever the
                   No. 3 in the Politburo says.

However, scientists and governments should avoid, at all costs, announcing that there is "no cause for concern." Five "no concerns" would
trigger the deep suspicion reflex, resulting in mass hysteria, a commission
of inquiry, and the resignation of the Secretary of State for the Environment. If you are too numb to cry, perhaps you can only laugh at the
Human Comedy.

And so the physical swirls of the Chernobyl cloud left behind swirls in
both the living environment and the human condition, and these disturbances played themselves out slowly along interconnected chains of life
and through interconnected human institutions. To understand these
effects we must move from the international scale of Europe down to the
national scale where we can see these effects in government institutions,
the academic world, and the lives of ordinary people. To do this we are
going to focus our "geographic lens" on two of the countries in western
Europe hit very hard by the Chernobyl disaster – Sweden and Norway –
not forgetting that even apparently disembodied "institutions" are actually made up of ordinary human beings who have to decide and to act in
some way when an event of the physical world suddenly impinges upon
their lives. At the center of many of those interconnected chains of effects
stands the ordinary person, that anonymous and somehow disembodied
"person in the street." Let one of them speak now, a young German
woman in Hamburg during those early days of anxiety, struggling to put
down her impressions in English for friends in America. She wrote then:

> On Friday [May 2] the cloud hang over Hamburg . . . as was announced by
> the *British* broadcasting . . . But people in Hamburg were not informed. As
> the sun was shining warmly, many people were lying in the sun. On
> Saturday the farmers were asked by the mass media to take the cattle away
> from the meadow. On Sunday it was severely advised not to go out in the
> rain, on Monday it was allowed that parents should not send their children
> to school . . . and the children should not touch the earth or plants outside.
> Imagine you are a child and you are forbidden to play in the open air and to
> touch the sand or flowers or leaves of trees . . . I will never forget the
> consciousness of the danger in these days. Even now it is difficult for me to
> write about it . . . So many things I took for granted before became precious
> to me, and I feel I get more and more ready to make personal sacrifices for
> the life of our wounded planet that needs so much healing, care and courage
> of people. I write this letter because Tschernobyl showed that we live on
> one earth.

And so it is to Sweden, a small part of our "one earth," that we now turn.

12 Sweden: Signals in the noise

In the words of the old Protestant prayer book it was "meet and right" that Sweden was the first to detect Chernobyl and sound the alarm for the rest of Europe. Ever since 1963, when the United States and the Soviet Union signed an agreement to stop nuclear tests above ground, Sweden has served as a sort of nuclear watchdog for the United Nations, and her network of highly sensitive radiation monitors has caught both the superpowers cheating twice. The network grew out of the work of Rolf Sievert, one of Sweden's pioneers in radiation physics, a man who pressed hard to monitor the fallout from scores of atomic bomb tests in the 1950s and 1960s. With her traditional stance of neutrality, Sweden has the trust of most countries, even though she has been subject to some pressure on occasion as the major powers stamped their diplomatic feet like spoiled and petulant children when they found that they could not get away with their deceit.

Sweden is a surprisingly large country – slide it down the map of Europe one whole length and southern Sweden would end up around Naples, Italy – with a small population of just over 8 million people. Starting as one of the most rigidly class structured societies of nineteenth-century Europe, she made an extraordinarily peaceful social, political, and economic transition into the twentieth century, and now enjoys one of the highest standards of living in the world. Yet for all its democratic openness Sweden is also a highly bureaucratized country, and perhaps it was no accident that she refurbished and modernized the old medieval position of *ombudsman*, a person "outside the system," to whom the ordinary citizen could appeal if an injustice or feeling of outraged impotence was generated by bureaucrats incapable of doing anything except "by the book." A small population also has its problems. In the upper echelons of the government, civil service, academic life, science and so on, everyone tends to know everyone else, and only rather small deviations from the expected way of doing things are tolerated. No one would be so crass as to say anything that might be construed as aggressive. It is just that you find yourself quietly frozen out and not invited to the right sorts of parties. This is no different from anywhere else, but it is often easier to accomplish.

Sweden is also highly dependent at the moment on nuclear power, with nearly half of her electricity coming from 12 atomic reactors at four power stations – Ringhals, Forsmark, Oskarshamn, and Barsebäck. These were built between 1972 and 1985, driven strongly by an intense national desire to become as self-sufficient as possible in the energy field. Atomic energy was the topic of enormous, and uncharacteristically acrimonious debate between nuclear scientists, businessmen, and government on the pronuclear side, and many people who felt strongly about the environment on the antinuclear side. After Three Mile Island the latter gained considerable strength, and in 1980 a national referendum was held with 60 percent of the people voting to use the reactors during their useful lifetime, but to phase out atomic power completely by 2010. Barsebäck is due to be closed down in the early 1990s, under considerable pressure from Denmark, whose Copenhagen lies just across the waters of the Öresund. But as the date gets closer more and more committees are appointed in Stockholm to "reconsider" the national referendum. A second referendum in which the people might express their wishes again is unthinkable to a Stockholm bureaucrat. Few have any doubts about the outcome after Chernobyl.

Just before Chernobyl many ordinary people's intuitive feelings about nuclear power, feelings heightened by Three Mile Island years before, were gradually dying down. After all, one reactor after another was being put into service without any problems, dependence on foreign oil was going down, the scientists and engineers said it was perfectly safe, stringent radiation monitoring was in place and confirmed that the scientists were right. Perhaps that referendum was too hasty and ill-informed? But the arrival of the Chernobyl cloud changed all that. We know now that it appeared silently over Sweden during the night of April 27 to trigger the alarms of Forsmark the next morning as people on the changing shifts carried fallout particles past the scintillation counters on their shoes. For the next three days a very uneven blanket of radionuclides – mainly iodine 131, caesium 134 and 137, and ruthemium 106 – fell in two great swaths in middle and northern Sweden (figure 4) centered on the towns of Gävle and Sundsvall. This remarkably detailed map, originally drafted at a much larger scale, was made not only from measurements at the 37 monitoring stations all over the country, but also from planes flying in a close scanning pattern with highly sensitive scintillometers picking up the long range gamma radiation from the fallout. If we could place this map over the one of rainfall, the match would be almost perfect.

When the cloud arrived every government department that could help was pressed into service – hydrology, meteorology, geology – as well as

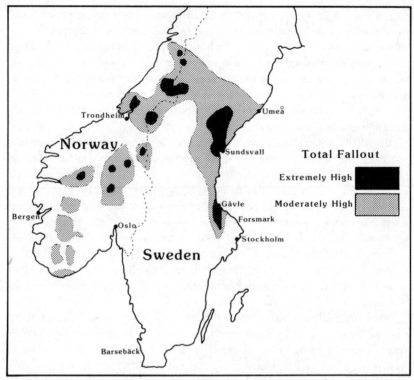

Figure 4 The general pattern of Chernobyl's fallout over Sweden and Norway. The areas of moderate and high intensity match the patterns of rainfall almost exactly.

the armed services, the universities, and the nuclear power industry itself. There is a capacity for concerted national action in Sweden that is difficult to match. Thanks to these remarkable scientific efforts, the basic pattern of fallout was quickly established, and many other critical facts besides. It was learnt, for example, that rainfall scavenging does not just increase fallout moderately, but produces a "washout ratio" (the ratio of radioactivity in the falling rain to the air) of up to 5 million. Even 1 millimeter of rain, just a brief drizzle, brings down particles that might otherwise have passed overhead. Sweden was actually hit twice, the second fallout roughly reinforcing the first. As the original "meteorological funnel" pointing to Scandinavia on Europe's pressure surface was blocked, the radioactive air swung further south over Europe. But then, just as the discharges at Chernobyl rose to the second peak, the air blocking Scandinavia moved on and the radioactivity streamed in a second time.

Although Sweden's combined scientific resources were marshalled with extraordinary efficiency and effect, the National Institute for Radiation Protection (NIRP) was unable to cope with the information requirements of the disaster. As in every other European country, few had foreseen the demands that would be made. "It was chaos on the information front," said one reporter, a "chaos" not helped by publications from the NIRP measuring radioactivity in nanograys, picocuries, microröntgens, and kilobecquerels, few of which were understood in terms of their scientific fundamentals, and none of which were meaningful in terms of their human consequences. In a rather admirable Swedish way of trying to get the facts on the table, Swedish Radio conducted a very thorough analysis of the information crisis during the first 40 days. It all came down to what a psychologist would call "cognitive dissonance," but we do not need any fancy term to understand that reassuring and disturbing news at the same time produces a sense of contradiction so that people become anxious and start worrying which information is right. Over half the people of Sweden had voted to phase out nuclear power, and many already had a gut feeling that the politicians, authorities, and experts did not really know what they were talking about. Now there were reports of radiation deaths, mass evacuations, women and children fleeing from Kiev, and daily reports of increasing radiation levels in Sweden itself. Two-thirds of the reports from television and radio were labelled "disturbing" – it is difficult to see how they could have been anything else – while one-third were classified as "reassuring."

Of all the "reassuring" reports half were made by the director of the NIRP, who was photographed wading through lush spring meadows with a Geiger counter telling the public that everything was under control and there was no cause for alarm. This was followed by an NIRP directive saying that the cows in the same meadows had to go back into the barn to be fed on pre-Chernobyl feed because iodine 131 in the milk was rising to unacceptable levels. Even so, the radiation was apparently so trivial that people could eat what they liked. Six days later restrictions were put on some vegetables, particularly parsley and chives with up to 7,700 bq and 4,000 bq/kg, and people were advised not to pick spring mushrooms. NIRP said it was perfectly safe for children to go outside and play on dusty football grounds and in sandboxes, and young conscripts were sent on military field exercises in the peak area around Gävle. At this time television was telling people that Austria was advising children and elderly people to stay indoors, and West Germany advising the same for pregnant women. Meanwhile the news programs showed farmers worrying about their crops and the cost of radiation-free fodder, and pregnant women worrying about cancer and the children they were carrying. Even the people officially designated to calm things down and give reassuring news had difficulties because it is not easy to be reassuring about catastrophic accidents and disturbingly high radiation levels. A careful linguistic analysis of what authoritative government personalities said shows an unusually high use of "attitudinal markers," words and phrases that betray the attitudes, preconceptions, and personal values of the speakers as they "reassured" the general public. Nevertheless, public trust was very thin at the end of it all.

This lack of trust must have been distressing to many scientists who felt that an enormous amount had been done under difficult and often pressing circumstances. They were quite right, for much had been accomplished. The monitoring system originally proposed in 1957 by Rolf Sievert had worked flawlessly, providing a stream of accurate information to the NIRP at Stockholm. Much of this information was used by the National Food Administration (NFA), which adopted the relatively stringent level of 300 bq/kg in all foodstuffs, and then started an extensive monitoring program that removed virtually all foodstuffs that came near such values. Cows were taken from pastures with high fallout, vegetables were monitored and taken off the market, and mushrooms were measured and people cautioned about picking them in the areas of heaviest fallout. Particular attention was paid to iodine 131 in milk, and so far as is known no milk products even approaching maximum levels appeared on the market. With a halflife of eight days the radioactivity disappeared quickly, and after six months of consistently low levels the monitoring program for milk was given up. All other monitoring of meat and vegetables, including game and wild berries, continued and was still in effect two years later. Particular attention was paid to the peak areas, particularly those that formed the home grounds of a remarkable group of people – the Sami (Lapps). For some of them the problems were especially severe, and we shall look at these later. Much of the information NFA had was summarized and made quickly available in Swedish. A month later English translations appeared so that others could see what was going on and learn from the experience. As far as the scientists were concerned, they provided the information, and in those early days and months it was used responsibly by those who had translated it into public food policies. There is no evidence to my knowledge that food even approaching these stringent maximum levels ever entered the "market food chain." Those who were responsible, both the scientists and the policymakers, must be given full credit.

But there are many food chains, and it is these that form some of the major long-term problems. Moreover they affect not just the human beings who are at the end of some of them, but all living creatures. The problem is that a food chain is really a powerful biological amplification

Much of the fallout was retained in lichen, a natural "air sponge", and a favourite food of the reindeer.

In Sweden and Norway the reindeer are slowly herded up along valleys to summer pasture in the high fjäll. At all times of the year they feed on the lichen, now a perfect repository for long-lived radioactive fallout.

The dams of Sweden's and Norway's hydroelectric programs have produced long lakes in the flooded, glaciated valleys, some of them former "villages" of the Sami. These could form "caesium sinks" if the fallout is retained in the bottom sediments.

Climbing from sea level in the fjords of Norway, through meadows to the high fjäll of the mountain backbone, was like climbing up a steep radioactive ladder.

Not everyone in Norway agreed that the technology associated with atomic power was a blessing.

system because each step in the chain concentrates the radioactivity at the step below it. In northern Sweden and Norway, for example, a lemming might eat berries and seeds covered with caesium fallout, and since small animals can eat their own weight in food quite quickly the caesium can concentrate to high levels, even in areas of only moderate fallout. Then the lemming might be caught by a gyrfalcon or snowy owl so that the caesium concentrated in its flesh is eaten by the bird. We already know the effects of such biological amplification in the case of DDT, which affected many birds of prey around the world. The peregrine falcon feeding on fish, birds, and rodents, and the Bermuda petrel feeding almost exclusively on fish far from shore in the open ocean, were nearly wiped out because DDT interfered with their shell-forming mechanisms. Many of the eggs laid had only a thin and easily torn membrane instead of a hard shell. The question is can we also trace similar effects of radioactivity as they are biologically amplified up these food chains?

So we come once again to that most difficult and general problem in so many scientific areas, the problem of "the signal in the noise." Can we point with some certainty either to specific cases where fallout has caused a fatality, malignancy or deformation, or to similar effects in large populations of living species? In the spring of 1987, a year after Chernobyl, some English ornithologists and birdwatchers thought that perhaps there had been a significant drop in fieldfares and redwings. These are thrush-like birds migrating in the early spring to eastern Britain from Scandinavia where they feed on winter berries and seeds. If these were heavily contaminated by fallout and eaten in large quantities – and there are not many grams of flesh in a fieldfare – then could the large amount of caesium in a small number of grams lead to absorbed doses high enough to kill detectable numbers? Could the lower counts of birds that first spring point to a real Chernobyl effect?

The problem is that bird populations in nature are notoriously variable, particularly for small migrating birds who one year might run into a storm over the North Sea and another year have clear skies and good tail winds. For 18 years now Swedish ornithologists have been making population counts in undisturbed areas of northern Sweden reserved for biological research, and the numbers of both these birds fluctuate so widely from one year to another that it is impossible to conclude whether the fallout had any effect. Sometimes short-term trends of bird counts were up, sometimes down. The background "noise" of natural fluctuations presently obscures any effect – if there is one. As for falcons, snowy owls, osprey and loons, most are protected for their current rarity or usefulness in controlling rodent populations, and no autopsies have been conducted.

The same is true for another beautiful wild animal, the otter, but here the "signal in the noise" problem gets even more difficult. All over Europe otter populations have been in devastating decline as chemical and other industries pour their pollutants into rivers, using them as sewers and waste conduits. The North Sea is the final receptacle for much of western Europe's filth, and many bottom fish are now hauled up with chemically induced cancerous lesions. The Baltic Sea provides a similar story, and throughout most of Scandinavia, and south through eastern Europe to Greece, the otter has virtually been eliminated. Today there is only a small group in Sweden to the east of Lake Vänern, and a few scattered populations in the mountains of the north still untouched by chemical waste. Like the seals of the Baltic, also in steep decline with cancerous lips, livers and deformities, the otter has been strongly affected by the chlorinated organic compounds, particularly the PCBs. Otters are royal animals in Sweden, and when their bodies are found they are sent to the National History Museum in Stockholm for examination. But no dead animals had been found that first year after Chernobyl, and there was revulsion at killing any of these lovely animals for examination. Both otters and seals consume large quantities of fish in relation to their own body weights, so they are already at the end of a powerfully amplified food chain.

How powerful exactly is that food chain amplification system that leads to the fish that are eaten by the otters and seals? And not just otters and seals, but birds of prey and you and me? Because people are at the end of that fish food chain we know quite a lot about it, and the way it amplifies radioactivity should give pause to anyone maintaining that there is no cause for alarm. Just off the east coast of Sweden, by Forsmark, a ring of small islands has been joined together to form an artificial lagoon. All of the cooling water from two of the atomic reactors at Forsmark, about 86,000 litres per second, is pumped via a tunnel into the lagoon, raising the temperature 8–10° C (14–18° F) higher than the surrounding Baltic. Gratings cover all the gaps to prevent fish from entering or leaving the square kilometer of lagoon water, and the site forms one of the finest biological testing stations of its kind in the world, totally open and welcoming to all types of research scientists. It was built by the atomic power authorities to monitor any radioactive discharges from Forsmark, discharges so small that they were almost unmeasurable. So innocuous were the cooling discharges, and so uncontroversial were the research findings, that the power station pulled out of the fish research business in 1985 and turned the whole facility over to Sweden's Environment Protection Board – producing considerable strain in the scientific budget.

Now when something like a Chernobyl happens it is very important to have "before and after" data, and this is where Forsmark showed that you never know in science when a piece of information is going to come in handy. The caesium 137 in seawater was carefully monitored at the test station, and the becquerels (per liter) rose from the barely measurable during May of 1986 to nearly 4 bq in June, declining thereafter to almost zero levels by next January. Even 4 bq are impossible to detect except with extraordinarily sensitive instruments, and by no stretch of the most anxious imagination could anyone worry about them. Presumably the water was getting minute quantities of caesium from river discharges, but it soon faded away. The problem is that minute animals called zoo- and phytoplankton pick up the caesium before they become food for small shrimps and other marine animals, which in turn become food for small fish, which become food for big fish. The result was that radioactivity in the muscle of perch in the Baltic went from practically nothing in May to 3,100 bq the following December, with the trend still rising sharply upwards. In other words in six months, starting with the most minute concentrations in the water, the food chain amplified the radioactivity by nearly three orders ($10 \times 10 \times 10$) of magnitude, or about a thousandfold.

As it turned out, these levels in Baltic fish, ten times the limit allowed for human consumption, became commonplace and almost derisory in freshwater fish, particularly predators like perch, pike, trout, and grayling, all prized by fishermen for their sport and taste. In lakes around the peak at Gävle you could easily trace what was happening. First the levels in the bottom-feeding bream started to rise from nothing to 1,000 bq during May, and by June they exceeded 2,000 bq. But by then the perch had been feeding on small bream minnows and had risen to 3,000 bq, shooting up to over 8,000 bq the next month with the predator pike quickly coming up behind them. By August the trend was firmly upward, pointing to over 10,000 bq by autumn before the lakes and rivers froze over. These levels were commonplace all over the north, with peaks as high as 27,349 bq that first August, and there was no evidence that things were any better the following spring. More than three years later many catches are more than 15 times the limits for human consumption, and some perch are 50 times over the limit.

Then a curious thing happened: suddenly, in the autumn, money for testing fish was cut off from Stockholm. This did not stop the tests completely, but anything further had to be undertaken by the communes themselves, the small areas of local government within the northern *län* or "counties." Many are rural and heavily forested areas, perhaps served by a small market town, and few had the sophisticated scientific equipment to measure caesium radioactivity. Nevertheless, thousands of samples of fish and meat (and even potatoes) were sent to major medical and technical centers where the tests were performed and the records carefully stored. The problem was that no one reported the continuing flow of data to Stockholm, data reporting 3,000–22,000 bq in fish all over the hard hit areas of the north. The result was that each testing center of a county kept meticulous item-by-item records – what a fish was, where and when it was caught – but no one was putting the total picture together. One radiophysicist said "People in Stockholm obviously don't want to know, and as for the locals, perhaps it's a bit like radon testing, a lot of them just don't want to find out. They all think 'what will the tourists say if the fish radioactivity is high?'." So no one has any idea about the overall picture, and perhaps some really do not want it. "We have all the data alright," said one physicist, "and anyone can see it if they want to. But we're physicists and don't really think about maps. Perhaps geographers should make such a data bank."

But when I posed this question to a prominent member of the NIRP he looked at me suspiciously and said "But what would you want such a data bank for?" I wanted to reply "But how can you really understand what is happening without it?" But the man had flown in from Stockholm that day to wave an NIRP pamphlet at a scientific meeting, and to add his voice to the phalanx of pronuclear scientists ready to denigrate any point of view that might raise alternative questions. It was obvious that nothing but resentment would be generated by such a reply. If you want a problem to go away, the last thing you need is Geographical Information Systems (GIS), a modern computerized databank containing all the observations you can find in their temporal and spatial coordinates. Physicists, who deal essentially with the dimensions of time and space should understand this for they stand in the heritage of Galileo and Newton and Einstein. All three would have understood the importance of such observations, but many of their inheritors informed by different "worlds" do not want to know. Too much is at stake "politically," including the politics of scientific reviews and research grants, in a small country where everyone knows everyone else and boat-rocking is not appreciated.

The fish food chain is a particularly powerful one not simply because of predator–prey relationships among the fish themselves, but because right at the beginning of the food chain are plants and animals that have an uncanny capacity for concentrating radioactivity. Many of them sieve and strain large amounts of water flowing past as they search for nutrients, and in doing so they absorbed the radionuclides in the water. The problem was the same with blue mussels in the Baltic, which hit 2,130 bq five months after Chernobyl, a level helped by a particular propensity to take up radioactive silver 110. This element came as a total surprise, because it did not appear immediately in the fallout, and seems to be a product of radioactive decay. It is causing considerable concern in Britain also, because it crosses the gut wall of mammals very easily, and then concentrates in the liver, spleen, and some of the eye tissues. In fresh water the mechanism is roughly the same only on a much smaller, microscopic scale. Even that first summer algae in some northern lakes hit 296,000 bq/kg, and in the high fjäll, the mountain backbone between Norway and Sweden, minute creatures called diatoms reached 300,000 bq from caesium. So far as is known, this is the highest level of radioactivity ever recorded in biological material. Diatoms form the food for freshwater zoo- and phytoplankton which are the food for small shrimp, and so on up the always-amplifying chain.

Unfortunately, it was impossible to get even small amounts of money to do this research, and the measurements on special and highly sensitive instruments had to be done by sympathetic friends in the military on "off duty" hours. The armed forces in Sweden have some of the finest and most advanced instruments in the world for measuring radiation. "We did it because no one else would do it," said one radiophysicist, who conducted some of the field investigations, "We thought it was important to find out, and fortunately we had a good fellow at the local level who let us count the two weeks as part of our duties." Another scientist tried through official national channels to get small research funds for testing lakes and rivers in the high *fjäll*, but the application was turned down. "We have to do it in private, almost in secret," said one young scientist, "otherwise we just get frozen out." Others have had similar problems, including some of Sweden's most distinguished scientists. One applied for research funds to study caesium removal, including the possibility that acid rain might interact with caesium fallout and make it easier to flush from the environment. It might also change it into a form that could penetrate the hard surfaces of some insects, so making them more vulnerable to smaller doses. Funds for this research were refused. Another scientist published a review of what was known at the time in an impeccable scientific journal, and commented that even small doses of radioactivity can disrupt rather sensitive aquatic systems, documenting the statement with a just-published study in an equally impeccable scientific journal. But Swedish reviewers thought that even this simple and well-documented statement was "too bold," and the editor demanded the removal of the offending sentence and the reference. A year later national and international commissions lowered "safe" levels three- to fivefold.

Sometimes even the best of intentions backfire because we cannot foresee the future. Hundreds of the long lakes in the north of Sweden are the result of her intensive hydroelectric policy over the past century, and the lake levels fluctuate as the melting snows from the mountains are stored in the summer, only to be used to turn electric turbines during the peak season in the winter. The result is that water levels are low in the spring and great ice wedges jam the uncovered shorelines. As these melt they carry vegetation to the bottom of the deep lakes where it lies, unavailable as nutrients for many fish. To overcome this problem scientists introduced a little biological "elevator" to lift the nutrients to higher levels so the fish could take advantage of them. The "elevator" was a small photonegative shrimp from southern Sweden. In the day time *Mysis relicta* shuns the light and descends to the bottom to feed on the deep rotting vegetation. Then at night he comes up plump and well fed, only to be eaten by fish which grow plump, and are then caught by people who are watching their weight. The problem is that the sediments of lake bottoms are a good place for fallout to settle, particularly if there are clays to bind it up in their lattices. Today *Mysis relicta* may be bringing up caesium that would otherwise settle in a safe place and be putting it back into the food chain.

But there are other food chains that end in human beings, and when these are disrupted a ripple of effects may move through other chains of people and institutions. Moose, for example, play an important role in several ecological systems, not the least as an important source of protein for many rural families in Sweden. Like many rural parts of the United States, where annual deer hunting is not just a sport but a necessary part of the household budget, Sweden also has a carefully regulated game management program that issues licenses and controls the annual culling of the large herds. But moose hunting has other important economic consequences, particularly for the huge national forestry program. Few outside of rural Sweden realize that if a forest is logged the law requires it to be replanted immediately by the owner. If it is not then the forestry commission will do it – and charge the owner an arm and a leg for its services.

It is at this point that the moose and the forest interact. When the newly replanted trees are very small the deep winter snows cover them completely and protect them from moose predations. In the summer the young trees are also safe since moose greatly prefer the new grasses and aquatic plants in the marsh areas. The problem comes when the trees are "moose-height," small enough to offer their top branches to hungry moose in winter, but not small enough to be buried and protected by the snow. Then moose can devastate a tree plantation, either killing the trees or greatly reducing their commercial value. It is for this reason that moose herds are kept at low but easily sustained levels, and in the absence of hunting the moose population can explode. This is the great fear today. During the first three autumns after Chernobyl much of the moose meat was registering well over the legal limits for consumption, and Sweden set up mobile testing stations – nicknamed the Becquerel Express – to help hunters test their kills in the field. Many had to be condemned, and in one *län*, Västerbotten, most of the 14,000 moose had to be buried in large pits. "What's the use," said one hunter, "of killing moose if we can't eat the meat?" Like many wild grazers, moose can scan a wide area as they feed, and there is a strong correlation between ground deposition and radioactivity in the meat, particularly for younger animals who take a high proportion of their food closer to the ground. To encourage hunters to keep trying, the costs of moose hunting were slashed, and if the meat tested at over 300 bq/kg a hunter was excused the testing fee.

Few think of insects forming part of a food chain ending in human beings, and most of the time they are regarded as a nuisance. Bees are probably the major exception, for everyone is familiar with the taste of honey, and many realize how important bees are for pollinating plants, especially fruit trees. During the first warm days of spring bees leave their hives and gather pollen from the newly emerging flowers, compressing the pollen into small yellow bundles on their legs and carrying them back to the hive to feed the larvae. Unfortunately, in the Gävle area the flowers had heavy depositions of fallout, and the bee larvae were feeding on pollen at 20–25,000 bq. The critical stage of development is during the 9th–14th day when the larvae undergo the process of metamorphism, changing their form from grubs to bees. A large sample of larvae had been collected from 140 beehives in the Gävle area, but all applications for modest research funds to undertake the patient analysis were denied by Stockholm. "The government seems to have lost interest," said one researcher, and the larvae had to be frozen and stored to wait until more favorable times came. Three years later they were still sitting there, the radioactivity, especially the radioactive iodine 131, decaying away.

This delay was a great pity, for there was already some evidence of dwarfing, bees emerging from the cells about the size of a small house fly. But this had occasionally been seen before, perhaps as a result of pesticides, and once more it became a matter of establishing a true Chernobyl effect, that signal in the noise. Much of the initial radioactivity in the pollen was from iodine 131, but this has now decayed almost away in the frozen larvae years later. As for the pollen, levels fell quite quickly so that monitoring measurements were discontinued over most of Europe by the middle of July. But one man in Sweden continued these studies and was able to show that another chain was involved. July was very wet that year, and by August the caesium had penetrated to the root zones of the fireweed and the heather, two favorite flowers for the bees gathering nectar. Radioactivity in honey now rose as the plants took up the caesium systemically, with levels in the Gävle area ten times that of the legal limits for sale. The next year the levels were even higher in the honey, and today it has become obvious that the caesium is in the root zone of the plants for many years to come. Each autumn the radioactivity shoots up to 3,000 bq/kg as the bees gather the late nectar from the heather.

There is no question that the town of Gävle and its immediate surrounds took the brunt of the fallout. The official map showed a peak over the town and labelled the shading "greater than 120,000 bq/m²," which was true, at least up to a point, for only gamma radiation was being recorded. The NIRP's own published measures per square meter for grass samples in the beginning of May showed a maximum of 750,000 bq, most of it iodine 131, but three weeks later it was still 575,700, most of it now consisting of caesium. Yet in the middle of all this (May 12, 1986), the NIRP was issuing general reassurances that children could go out of doors and play in sandboxes. One school principal, after telephoning health "experts" who took their cue from Stockholm, let children go on a school picnic where there were games and roughhousing in the dry woods and dusty fields. Many Gävle mothers were deeply disturbed, and I remember vividly a year later sitting around a table with a number of them, all professionally qualified in their own work, and listening to their outraged and anxious comments. What particularly angered them was that the children of Forsmark employees, and the children of science faculty at Uppsala University, children of two groups who presumably knew their radiobiology, had been strongly advised to stay indoors during those early days. This was at the time that the women at Gävle were watching television for every scrap of information they could get, and the spokesmen for the NIRP were saying that there was no danger at Gävle, no need to stay indoors and, of course, no real cause for alarm. "How could they do it?", said one mother, "How could they say that? And that 'expert' who came here from Forsmark to reassure us . . . even he didn't dare to come out and say it was 'not dangerous' when we really pressed him for answers!"

Gävle was also the place where young conscripts in the Swedish army were sent on field exercises, running through grass loaded with fallout and breathing dust close to the ground as they went through infantry maneuvers. Assured by the experts that no harm could possibly come from these exercises, and perhaps even placed there to demonstrate how "innocuous" even the peak area of the fallout was, the maneuvers were not treated kindly by a foreign radiation expert in a rather intense dialogue with the dirctor of the NIRP.

Visiting doctor	I wouldn't send young men in there [Gävle] to have a military exercise. I think that's crazy to be lying on the ground, rolling around and raising the dust and breathing it in. That's no place to have a military exercise if it's your high fallout area.
Director	It depends on the levels you have in the area, right?
Visiting doctor	Well, from the map I saw of Sweden that looked like the worst place to pick for a military exercise. It's the high fallout area. You don't send young men in there that are of reproductive age.
Director	I think that's going a bit too far ... because we're still dealing with radiation doses on the order of a millisievert.
Visiting doctor	And you think that's nothing!
Director	Yes, yes, no, you, you, well you are aware that there might be some injury with it but you try to be reasonable in what you're doing against it.
Visiting doctor	I don't consider it reasonable to expose ...
Director	We have areas in Bohuslän [southeastern Sweden] where the mean gamma levels are four times normal.
Visiting doctor	You're not hearing me ... that doesn't justify saying a fallout area is just the same as some other [area] people are living in and therefore I won't say anything or therefore I'll send in a military group for an exercise!

Once again there was confusion among those who should have known better between background radiation, with a high proportion of gamma that hardly enters the food chain, and fallout breathed into lung tissue or swallowed into the stomach. Then the beta and heavily weighted alpha particles have to be considered for the severe damage they can do to living cells. Computing millisieverts and failing to think further is not enough.

People were numbed by the high radiation readings, the conflicting reports, and the inevitable rumors that made it increasingly difficult to tell the true from the false. In the face of a silent enemy it was difficult to know how to respond. Only a year before Sweden's Prime Minister, Olof Palme, had been murdered in cold blood as he walked home with his wife from a movie in Stockholm. Even today fresh flowers lie and are renewed on the place where he fell. It was a traumatic event for the people of Sweden – "things like that just don't happen here," they said – and in many schools, including Gävle's, the children were encouraged to talk about it, to collect information, even to put out a small newsletter for their fellow pupils. These sorts of expressions were deliberately designed by the teachers to be cathartic for the children. But "cathartic" is from the old Greek *katharos*, pure, and its verb form meaning to cleanse or to purify. Aristotle uses it to describe the effects of tragedy, the release from tension. Nothing like that happened with Chernobyl, in fact quite the opposite. Few teachers had enough knowledge to help the children, and many were unable to release the anxiety and tension that they themselves felt. A number of the women felt what they called a "conscious silent making" on the part of the government. "We just felt an incredible sadness," said one woman. "You look forward to the spring, to the flowers and mushrooms and berries . . . and now it seemed all 'dirty' so that you were afraid of it." The anxiety also showed up in the local hospital. One young woman, pregnant with her first child, was so distraught that she was advised by doctors to leave the area until her child was born. A local farmer, thinking his fields were permanently contaminated, and feeling sorry for his poor animals who could not leave their barns for the bright spring meadows, developed a severe psychosis and had to be treated in the psychiatric ward. A second farmer could not bear to see his "world" destroyed, his whole life on the land shattered, and took his own life, deciding to be no more.

"Yes, but these are extremes," say those who compute and declare there is no cause for alarm. "The fact that these people entered psychiatric wards and killed themselves shows that they were crazy." Human perceptions, emotions, and feelings do not form part of the arithmetic, and they are difficult to capture in the thinking of a person whose "world" is a measured and formally related mathematical place. You have to leave your Stockholm office, go about the world, and talk to people with a strong dose of ordinary commonsense. Most of them are quite willing to do arithmetic, but they also want to trust the results. Their world is real too, and when an instinctive trust is broken between their world and yours, it is not easily replaced. "I just don't understand it," said one radiophysicist in a rather hurt voice at a scientific meeting, "we know what we're doing, so why don't people trust what we say?" "Because," said a forthright geneticist, "Because you're the ones who have been telling people it couldn't happen, and now it has. Why are you surprised that they don't trust you anymore?"

It is a matter of trust, and the lines that are drawn divide people into those who are trusted and those who are not. In the course of writing this book I could almost invariably tell within 30 seconds "where someone was coming from." Before one interview with a distinguished oncologist (cancer specialist) a geneticist said to me quietly "Don't say anything, just let him do the talking. I think you'll learn a lot." It was easy advice to follow, for he took over from the first moment, and with a voice full of scorn and pity for those who were ignorant, demonstrated on the back of an envelope (I have it to this day as a souvenir), that precisely one-third of one Swede would contract cancer as a result of Chernobyl's fallout. But I had just been talking to the Sami in Gäddede, another fallout peak in the mountains along the Norwegian border, and I knew what the becquerels were in reindeer meat, fish and local berries, all staple foods for these people. No good spatially averaging all that away with a hundred farmers from Skåne in southern Sweden. Why stop there? Why not average reindeer herders with Portuguese fishermen? I did not trust the nonsense on the back of the envelope, and I could not bring myself to trust the man.

Sweden faces a great tension today, one that arises out of deeply held convictions that are essentially scientific and technical on one side, and intuitive and instinctive on the other. There is in Sweden, and in all Norden countries, a very deep and informing ethos, an ethical stance towards nature that is difficult to convey in words. It is informed by love, by a deep sense of gratefulness for natural beauty, and it is translated into a sense of caring and responsibility that is captured by the old English words "husbandry" and "stewardship." It is instilled very early: small children, only three or four years old at a *barndaghem*, a little pre-kindergarten "school," are often taken on nature walks in fair weather, through parks and meadows, through springtime woods marked with the royal crown, the old sign that these quiet and beautiful areas belong to everyone today – and are everyone's responsibility. There is nothing "heavy" about this, no admonishments, no lectures. Just a quiet and natural absorbing of the sense of care that comes out later in small signs like *Håll Naturen Ren* (Keep nature clean and pure), and *Respekt för Fjället* (Respect the mountains) – for what they are in all their beauty, and for what they can do to you if you are incautious. Mushrooming and berry-picking are old and cherished delights still informed by medieval customary law that allows all to wander freely to pick anything below waist height, providing you respect the rights of others and shut the gates behind you, of course. Many have *sommerstuga*, summer homes in the countryside to which whole and remarkably extended families flee in summer – when Scandinavia almost closes down. Many placed salt lickstones in the forest that first summer for the animals, hoping that the sodium and potassium would block the uptake of the caesium. The care shows in the banning of billboards in Sweden, despite commercial protests that business would plummet, because the beauty of a wayside landscape belongs to all. The care shows in Norway's banning of snowmobiles, except for rescue work and reindeer herding, because the forests are a source of tranquility, of true re-creation for all. The care shows in a marvellous book by a Swedish ecologist and an artist recreating the way four rural landscapes came to be, and what they might look like in the future under alternative energy policies. Most of the first printing was sold to the National Farmers Association of Sweden, and other printings followed quickly.

The scientific and technical convictions are often equally sincere, and almost by definition lie at levels of authority and power in government, industry, and science that interlink in both formal and informal ways. Producing nearly 50 percent of Sweden's electricity, the nuclear power industry, a state–private–public service consortium, wields a strong influence by the way it employs public relation firms, using them to point to its own, almost impeccable record and its willingness to adopt and pioneer safety devices and precautions. "It simply couldn't happen here," said one of them, "Swedish engineering wouldn't let such a thing occur." In Scandinavia, as elsewhere, the old gods have fled, and *hubris* is no longer in the modern scientist's vocabulary. Many in the industry feel a deep sense of injustice that their industry and their own professional lives are due to be phased out by 2010. A number in the civil service agree with them, and are worried about where the energy is going to come from. Government publications have titles like "We Are Not As Radioactive As You've Been Led to Believe," and "Where On Earth Do You Get The Energy From?"

But the scientific debate is informed by the scientists themselves, and the most authoritative, and therefore the most powerful, are in the Swedish Academy of Sciences. Many are from physics and chemistry and other sciences dealing with the physical world, a material world which simply lies there to be structured and understood and does not answer back in "irrational" ways. You do not measure human love and caring and meaning, and despite the claims of certain psychologists, who were never taught what *psyche* means, these lie beyond the rulers and the relating that make up the world of physical science. The result is that 80 percent of the members of the Swedish Academy of Sciences are pronuclear, often very strongly so, feeling that Sweden would be virtually committing national suicide if she closed down her nuclear power plants. It is these convictions, sincerely held and rationally computed, that inform the attitudes, the research judgements, and the advice given. It is to these opinions that senior civil servants in Stockholm listen, and it is these opinions from experts that one relies upon if one has no expertise oneself. If you desperately want a national problem to go away you listen to those who say there is no problem. And it helps if no one can marshal conclusive evidence that anyone has been hurt because the background noise effectively smothers the signal.

Not that the scientific opinions are always consistent and free of contradiction. You would think that the immediate response of a scientific academy to a catastrophic event lying between those physical and human worlds would be to call an emergency conference of physical, biological, and human scientists. Science exists to lighten the darkness, and nature does not wait for a review process of research proposals that is properly careful and conservative under normal circumstances. These procedures only appear ponderous and cast a shadow when action has to be taken quickly. "We would have had such an emergency conference a few years ago," said one distinguished member of the Academy to me, "but then we had scientific leaders who would make such a decision and take the responsibility for it." But perhaps if all your preconceptions are pronuclear they inform such possibilities into the realm of indecisiveness. The result was caution not action, with the result that no decisions were taken to set in motion highly imaginative and coordinated research programs, some of which should have been supported and put into effect immediately. In times like these you need a little "risk capital," funds to support research outside the usual channels. The NIRP made the claim that it was supporting "lots of research . . . we have spent millions of crowns" said one official. Some of it was useful. None of it could have rocked the boat. *Quis custodiet ipsos Custodes?*

Nor were individuals always consistent. One member of the Academy who held high office, a physicist who was strongly pronuclear, provided one of the finest examples of the NIMBY-NOOS complex ever seen. NIMBY-NOOS is a grave inconsisto-contradicto-malady that is difficult to diagnose before it strikes with great swiftness, otherwise known as "not-in-my-back-yard" or "not-on-our-street." Owning a summer home on Sweden's south coast, and hearing that an atomic power station might be built nearby, he declared that he would sell out at once and leave if the plans for the damned thing went through.

Nor are all scientists dedicated to lightening the darkness too much if their preconceptual instincts inform their scientific interpretations too strongly. One physicist reported blandly that radiation levels in some of the fish in mountain lakes exceeded 300 bq/kg, which was quite true because *average* readings in some *län* were six times as high, with peaks at 48,000 bq. Most reasonable people would agree that these values exceed 300. The same person noted that some reindeer meat had been tested at "several thousand becquerels," which was also quite true, but raised the question of what he meant by "several" when the tests were measuring peaks of 8,000 bq in the *län* he was referring to, but 16,400 bq and 15,400 bq in those next door during the early months, values that would rise close to 100,000 bq later. There appears to be some temptation to be "economical with the truth."

There is also a tendency in science to see only what you are looking for, and this may be conditioned by how you are prepared to look. Many advances in science and understanding come from serendipity effects, when something suddenly comes to light which was not suspected before. Radiophysicists from one Swedish university, who were also associated with the nuclear industry, searched for radioactive hot particles that were produced when the initial explosion at Chernobyl pulverized the fuel rather than melting it. Using standard volumes of air passing through filters they detected one or two. But a highly respected radiophysicist from Finland, working under the same scientific conditions, detected 10,000 particles using special film and three days of exposure time. He pointed out that some were pure uranium and ruthenium capable of killing cells in lung and other tissue completely within 0.1 millimeters, and damaging others with their alpha particles up to 7 millimeters away. "In petri dishes," he said, "you can see the clear regions of dead cells with the naked eye." Paradoxically, the danger arises not so much from the dead cells, because the body quickly tries to repair such small chronic lesions. The main danger is to the cells outside of the small spherical "killing ground" around the particle where the cells are only wounded. It is these damaged cells that can turn malignant, and it was in these that genetic changes in RNA were observed. For those who like to compute probabilities, it makes a difference if the number of particles is two or 10,000.

Once again, the swirling cloud that brought the fallout to Sweden produced swirls and eddies in the biological and human condition below it, and these effects moved over natural and human structures made up of connections between living things and human institutions. We separate these only for descriptive convenience, because language constrains us to a chain-like narrative and we have to cut into the interconnected story somewhere. But conceptually, when we think about these things, we separate the structures carrying the transmitted effects at our peril. "Out there" the structures of the physical, biological, and human worlds are all connected together. The effects of caesium do not stop at the end of biological food chains, but cross over to the structures of human institutions. Here new chains of connections, made up of interconnected people and the institutions they form, carry the effects, and these effects may well alter in turn the human structures that carry them. The final effects are always political. The caesium buck stops at the body politic.

Chernobyl revived the nuclear power debate in Sweden as perhaps nothing else could have done. An event thousands of kilometers away was not a "remote" event that you read about one day and promptly forget the next, but something that landed on your own doorstep and insinuated itself into your daily life. And yet for the most part it was invisible, and perhaps all the more frightening for that. "Fear can be more damaging than radiation," said the pronuclear people in response to a surge of antinuclear feeling. And perhaps they were right? How shall we, quite concretely, ever find out when that signal is buried so deeply in the noise? But the hope of a democracy is that ordinary people do not put aside their commonsense, and if they demand caution then even a powerful Establishment protected by bureaucratic bastions must listen.

Quite apart from its external neutral stance, Sweden maintains a respectful and respected balance in her own political affairs. Dominated by the Social Democratic Party for 44 years, with the Center, Liberal, Conservative and a gaggle of smaller parties in opposition, Sweden shifted in 1976 to a coalition led by the Center Party which had committed itself against nuclear power. Three Mile Island had already produced second thoughts and considerable stress and strain within the parties supporting nuclear power, and the upshot was the 1980 referendum that required a phasing out by 2010. The fires were banked, but still they burned: the winds of Chernobyl only fanned political embers that were still glowing. The result was that the Environmental Party, the Greens, a party of little political significance, gained considerable support. If an election had been held a year after Chernobyl the polls showed that 7–8 percent of the Swedish people would vote for them, and given the delicate balance of power between the other parties, the Greens might well have made the difference in forming a workable majority or not. Given their own commitment to environmental issues, there is no question that the price of cooperation would have been greater attention to environmental issues of all sorts. Thus do 2 kilograms of caesium distributed over a map tip the scales of political institutions.

But the effects of the physical world on the human depend on how those human institutions are structured and situated. Situated not simply in geographic space, but situated in cultural, political, and economic "spaces." Different countries, different "systems," respond in different ways. The cloud rose over the mountains separating Sweden and Norway, and down came the rains on Norway too. Yet the response was quite different. As we shall see.

13 Norway: Do it and we'll find the money

Compared to Sweden, Norway is a warm country. Her coastline is continuously washed by the Gulf Stream, so that even that portion far above the Arctic Circle is tempered by the great movement of energy that was first captured from the sunlight in the Caribbean. On earth satellite pictures you can see the huge whorls and eddies of warm water swirling northwards like nature's tankers delivering heat to an otherwise frozen and desolate shore. Move due west from Norway's North Cape and you come only to "Greenland's icy mountains." For over a millennium Norway's outlook has been west and south towards that warming sea.

She is also a country of awesome beauty that makes glad the heart of man and leads to reflection on that which is good. Her landscape is one of mountains limned in sparkling light, and rivers of ice cold water rushing to deeply incised fjords. Her 3 million people nestle deep in the ice-scoured valleys, or gently tame a land the ice has left behind. Distances on the map bear little relation to conventional travel times, for the roads twist and turn up the steep gradients, only to be broken by the long fingers of the fjords carrying the warm seawaters deep into the heart of the country. If you want to move north and south, and you are not in a hurry, you had better do it in the old way and take a boat. In winter even the main road between Norway's major cities, Oslo and Bergen, closes down, and travel is along a rail line kept open by enormous ploughs cutting a canyon through the snow. In Norway you can feel the isolation, and know the tranquility that comes with it.

Despite the feeling of disconnection, there is a fierce national pride and sense of unity, although not always agreement about the best course to steer. A member of NATO, Norway voted to stay out of the Common Market, splitting herself from Denmark in the process, but remaining in a traditional Nordic alignment with Sweden. The national referendum pitted the young and rural against the middle-aged urban, and the young and rural won in the full knowledge of the economic price they might pay for keeping some control over their own destiny. That destiny includes oil and gas fields in the North Sea and hydroelectricity to burn. There is no atomic power; it has not even been contemplated except by a handful of engineers near Oslo who feel slightly chagrined at being left out.

No atomic power, no need for any institutions to inspect and control what you do not have. No reactors for atomic power, no need for a

National Radiation Protection Board. No chance of a nuclear accident, no need for any monitoring network. It is the Swedes next door, going hell for leather into the atomic stage, who need that, said the Norwegians. Norway had only a few monitors recording the radioactivity of the air, all associated with two small reactors in the south used solely for research in physics. Perhaps if any country in western Europe was unprepared it was Norway, despite the fact that other pollutants like acid rain had drenched her forests and killed her fish for many decades. Norway was no stranger to what rain clouds can bring. No country in Europe was really prepared to deal with Chernobyl, but there was an innocence to Norway's stance and trust that appears almost childlike in the all-knowing light of hindsight.

The first inkling came on April 28, a radio announcement that the Swedes thought they had had an accident at Forsmark. The now usual information crisis followed for the now usual reasons: the impossible, or at least the so unlikely that it might just as well be impossible, had happened. But never mind, it was far away said the Norwegian health authorities, trying to spread calm by indicating there was no cause for alarm. There is no reason to panic, and anyway iodine 131 decays to half strength in eight days, and there is no fallout north of Tunset (a town halfway between Oslo and Trondheim, Norway's third largest city). This, as it turned out, was totally false and could not have been based on any concrete information. In the early days there was very little information about the impact in Norway, and news from abroad came through the newspapers. "What other source could we have had," said one scientist. "We could only read the newspapers and listen to television like everyone else."

Then Norway's Geological Survey started its own monitoring program, measuring radioactivity on the ground, trying to piece together what had happened. It was slow work, taking 270 soil samples, some from remote and difficult areas, and it took a number of weeks, but working with the meteorologists the full impact at last became clear. The radioactive cloud that hit Sweden had been lifted by the mountains marking much of Norway's border, only to collide with an eastward movement of air from the Atlantic that was later to block the stream from Chernobyl and send it south over the rest of Europe. But over Norway the violent mixing and turbulence brought down the rain. Sometimes the gods are not kind, and Loki must have been in a particularly truculent mood. At some meteorological stations less than a millimeter was recorded in a single hour during the first and critical 48 hours, but it came at the height of the radioactivity and scavenged the particles to the ground. The map of rainfall and the map of fallout fit like a glove in three major patches: south–central Norway, the Trondheim area, and a large region in the mountains about 200 kilometers to the north, a major "homeland" for the Sami living in Norway. Over many hundreds of square kilometers the radioactivity on the ground exceeded 200,000 bq/m^2.

Trondheim is the site of Norway's Nature Conservancy Board, and also of one of Norway's major universities. While there was little in the way of "radioecological" research in Norway's biological sciences, there was a long and scientifically excellent tradition in botany and zoology grounded in direct field work and close observation. Above all, Norway's scientists know a great deal about what they call the "food web," the phrase itself indicating a perceptive awareness of the many interconnections between the chains of living things. Lemming specialists from Oslo, moss and lichen specialists from Bergen, reindeer specialists from Trondheim, and many other scientists of the living world were asked to help. Planning and coordination happened somehow, although to this day the director of the research is not quite sure how. On June 6, only five weeks after the cloud passed over, a telephone call came from the city's veterinarian. A redtailed deer killed by a car had been examined, and 2,800 bq/kg were in its muscles. A heavy traffic of caesium was already moving on and through the food web. Plans were made immediately to push the sampling of wildlife both on a local and national level, but in the middle of the scientific preparations a journalist from a small local newspaper got wind of the deer measurements and published the "story."

Then all hell broke loose, and a small scientific esablishment responsible for research, public education, administration, and a dozen other related functions found itself at the eye of an information storm. For three months at the Nature Conservancy Board the telephone hardly stopped ringing. Summer vacations were cancelled, and somehow the research and planning were done in the other 10 of the 16 hours of work each day, week in and week out, weekend in and weekend out. It was an extraordinary effort by a group of dedicated ecological scientists, and one that was backed to the hilt. Research, equipment and field supplies cost money – lots of money. In the first few weeks the annual budget was blown. "I hadn't the faintest idea where the money was coming from," said the research director, "I just made agreements and signed the bills. But we picked up the telephone, talked to the Minister of the Environment and she came through." The response from Oslo was immediate. "Do whatever you think is necessary, and we'll find the money," she said, and she was as good as her word. When the dust had settled, and the cost totalled up, the Norwegian parliament passed a special appropriation to cover all the extra expenses, and at the same time put "Chernobyl research" on a firm financial footing until 1990. No hesitation, just do it. No atomic power, no informing and shaping preconceptions. No atomic power industry, no pressure, no hiring of public relations firms to change images. No withholding of funds from biological scientists ready to help in anyway they could. Just do it – and we'll find the money.

And so they got to work, in the great mountains of southern Norway, in the wild country east of Trondheim, and in the home of the Sami along valleys in the north. Piece by piece the evidence came to light, most of it by sheer hard work in the field, some of it by luck. On the eastern fringe of the southern fallout zone an experimental station at Atna investigating acid rain was already in operation sampling rainfall, stream water, and soils several times a day. It provided important "before-and-after" measurements, and recorded nearly 15,000 bq/litre from iodine, barium, and caesium at the peak of the fallout. At Atna the soils were poor in nutrients, but on the northern edge of the same patch another station at Knutshø had soils that were relatively rich. Research was immediately started to see the way in which different soils affected the movement of caesium into the food web. The Norwegians were perhaps the first to investigate thoroughly the idea that soil composition and structure were major determinants in locking up or releasing caesium to plants, something that the British would realize a year later when models calibrated on clays gave totally misleading results when applied to upland soils.

Water . . . soil . . . vegetation . . . insects . . . earthworms . . . small birds . . . preying birds . . . animals . . . and from each "node" in the web other webs and chains branch off. Three subwebs were chosen for the research program into the 1990s. The first was that which connected the soil to birds and animals of prey. Woodcock, for example, feed largely on earthworms and insects of the soil. Within a few months most samples were over 1,000 bq., some as high as 3,500. Ptarmigan, birds of the high *fjäll*, were the same, and provided one more piece of evidence for the almost perfect correlation between fallout and altitude. A walk from the sea to the mountains was like climbing up a straight and steep radioactive ladder. It was the same with small animals feeding on caesium-soaked vegetation, but by chance the lemmings were at a nadir in their 11-year cycle, and 2,000 traps only yielded four rather bedraggled animals. Lemmings are a source of food for birds and animals of prey, particularly the roughlegged hawk, but more is being learned each day as the research program continues.

A second focus of the program is the "waterlife web," that potent amplification system we have already seen at work in the Baltic and on the high *fjäll* of Sweden. It has two major chains to it: one for the bottom feeders, either waterplants taking up caesium systemically from the bottom sediments, or animals feeding on them; the other for those taking the radioactivity directly from the water itself. The first runs through the small shrimps, water plants, and insects directly to trout and water birds – ducks, geese, loons, waders, and all who feed by the water's edge. Only ten weeks after the Chernobyl cloud, trout in the Hoysjoen (the "high lake") east of Trondheim were registering up to 25,456 bq, hardly surprising when the stomach contents were over 19,000 bq. Mayfly were the main food, and at the inlet to the Hoysjoen hatching mayflys were at 4,900 bq. Those at the outlet showed 18,500 bq. The animals whose food chain started at the bottom fared only slightly better. Char peaked at nearly 8,000 bq, and birds like the moorhen and young ducks were the same, mainly because the plants they feed on were up to 13,000 bq, both from surface contamination and radioactivity brought up systemically.

The third thrust of the research program links lichens with wolverines, foxes, and ravens, and in between stands a biological amplifier we shall examine much more closely when we look at the plight of the Sami. It is the reindeer, in southern Norway a truly wild animal like the roedeer or moose, hunted not herded, and an important source of food for other wild animals including (?) man. A single wolverine will take six reindeer in a winter, with the foxes and weasles picking up the leftovers, and the ravens clearing up afterwards. On the high Dovrefjäll of southern Norway the wild reindeer pawing through the snow in winter were eating lichens at 124,000 bq and absorbing 37,000 bq into their muscle tissue, amounts easily exceeded farther north in the Sami areas. In the summer, as the biological halflife of caesium in the reindeer fell from three weeks to one, and the diet changed to include new grasses, the radioactivity also fell, only to rise to even higher levels the following winter. The caesium was not moving out. One expert, a leading authority with 20 years of close field observation, felt that there were many more spontaneous abortions among reindeer, but impressions are not publishable science. How do you marshal evidence for the rates of spontaneous abortions in wild animals? How do you record them before? How after? Nevertheless, the finely honed impressions of a careful and experienced field observer are not to be set aside lightly, even if the signal remains hidden in the noise. Particularly worrisome is a possible connection between radioactivity levels in reindeer and the ability of their immune system to cope with other dangers. During the atomic tests of the 1960s the huge arctic explosions by the Soviets on Novaya Zembla laced Norway's northern province of Finnmark with fallout, particularly strontium 90 that goes straight to the bone and irridates the marrow producing blood corpuscles. Ten years later 20,000 reindeer died from a parasitic illness that normally they seem to be able to cope with. Today a major concern of this third research thrust is to monitor reindeer in the hard hit areas closely, taking blood samples and leucocyte counts. Learning from the "experiment" will continue far into the future. Nor does the effect of Chernobyl stop in the wildlife and reindeer. Two and a half years after the cloud passed over Norway radioactive levels in sheep grazing on the high *fjäll* started to rise to unacceptable levels. In many parts of Norway the sheep are driven each summer to the high pastures, and it is in these areas that the caesium is now working its way systemically up the grass stems that the sheep graze. "There doesn't seem to be any way of getting around it," said one farmer as he thought about breaking age-old habits of sheepraising, "And the cost of finding additional feed down here may be more than we can bear." Meanwhile the caesium cycles and recycles with the growing grass, but decays at its own 28 year halflife rate.

The contrast with Sweden requires no comment. With no commitment to atomic power and its powerful industry, Norway was able to respond to the scientific questions forced into view by the environmental "experiment" in a mutually supportive effect by her scientists and government that barred no line of investigation. With smaller resources, but high levels of scientific skills, the program moved with speed, with the major decisions being made by the scientists themselves, unhampered by the bureaucratic molasses of "appropriate channels." "It's easy enough for them," said one Swede, "They have no energy problem." Quite true, but such a comment only heightens the relation between science and the social matrix in which it is embedded. We shall have to look at this again.

But Norway and Sweden do face one similar problem, and it is proving a difficult one to solve. With Finland (and a small part of the Soviet Union), Norway and Sweden are the ancestral home of the Sami. Or, the Sami might say, our land, our ancestral home, became colonized as part of Norway and Sweden. And for the Sami, the reindeer are more than just a link in a food chain. They are the staff of life, the biological and material ground of a unique culture. Let us see what happened.

14　The Sami: How do we survive?

We call them the Sami, for that is their name. The more common word
"Lapp" has a derogatory connotation for many younger Sami, and what
greater right do a people have than to name themselves for others? They
are an ancient people, maintaining their identity since their long migrations across the roof of the world in pre-Christian times. Tacitus wrote of
them with respect, admiring their ability to lead a nomadic life in the cold
regions so far from his warm Mediterranean. When, rather importantly
and precisely, they peopled northern Finland, Norway, and Sweden, and
drove a wedge of settlement south along the mountain spine, is something
discreetly skirted by the modern governments. "We do not really know"
say the governments, with an eye to legal niceties, court cases and
prescriptive territorial rights. The result is that the Sami follow archaeolo-
gical work in their areas attentively, for dating a grave with obvious Sami
burial objects is evidence of occupance difficult to refute. The Swedes
themselves only pushed north and into the mountains in comparatively
recent times, jostling the old gods aside with their new Trinity.

Today you can forget the picture book and poster images of the Sami.
They are on their way out, particularly in the past ten years. "I can hardly
believe the changes I have seen since working with them over fifteen
years," said one Swedish museum curator who lived and worked with
them in the far north and learnt their language. Today the traditional gray
blue clothing with bright red trim so enhancing of Kodachrome is usually
put away for a few festive occasions each year. Now snowmobiles stand
in the yards of wooden houses, cars fetch supplies from the small service
towns, television brightens long arctic nights, and helicopters sometimes
help in the autumn roundups. Sami children receive the usual minimum
of nine years of primary schooling in Swedish, with four hours of Samisk
each week in the regular district schools, or they may attend one of seven
special schools where Samisk is the major language of instruction. The
choice is up to the parents. Today Sami are found in medicine, law,
education, and many other professions, but there is a concerted effort to
maintain a sense of identity. This is not always easy. Three different
languages, intermarriage, television, and a host of other smaller but
insinuating aspects of the larger cultures – Norwegian, Swedish, and

Finnish – draw the young people of a small culture into the orbit of a larger world. It is the old problem of identity and difference. When you lie in an in-between world, acknowledging differences and torn between identifications, symbols become of consuming importance. Those symbols are the herders, only about 10 percent now of the roughly 15,000–17,000 Sami in Sweden today, and about the same proportion in Norway's larger group of about 40,000. The Sami may be settling in permanent homes, the reindeer sleds may be giving away to snowmobiles, but the spirit of Sami culture still crystallizes in that old herding life that renews the annual cycle centuries old. If this is not understood, the rest will make no sense. We may see a quaint and charming people, as we are tempted into the gentle smile of misplaced condescension, but we shall not understand. That herding life, and those who hold to it, form the nexus of Sami culture. This is where it all comes together. If they go, so does the culture as it has maintained its identity and difference, its human integrity, over the centuries.

And at the center of that life are the reindeer. First hunted, later tamed, the reindeer supplied milk and meat and transportation and clothing and myths, and the stories sung-chanted in the long winter nights as a "yoiking" older generation passed the oral heritage to the next. Without the reindeer and their herders the material culture of the Sami disappears into objects displayed on a tourist's stall, and the spiritual culture becomes an ever-fainter memory as each new generation feels the heritage slipping from its grasp. It will happen, in the fullness of time it will inevitably happen, but it should be allowed to happen without the shock of looking into its dying eyes.

Traditionally, and that still means up to a few decades ago, reindeer herding was relatively intensive, the small herds moving from winter pastures in the low valleys to the high summer pastures of the *fjäll*, with all the family going along. A Sami "village" referred to the elongated territory following the valley into the high mountains. Today the old spring and autumn encampments tend to become the sites of permanent settlement in wooden houses, and the reindeer are allowed to roam freely, only being herded into corrals in the autumn for the annual slaughter. Having walked and driven across the high *fjäll* and down into the wooded valleys, I asked one 17-year-old herder "How do you find them? How do you know where they are?" He looked surprised in a polite sort of way and said "Oh we just feel where the wind is . . . and we know where they are." There is an attunement between the herders and their animals that must be respected, even when, perhaps especially when, it throws out a possibility not immediately accepted by modern veterinary science.

So where is the danger? It is the caesium in the lichen, a favorite food of the reindeer, one of the few animals capable of digesting this strange plant. Lichen does not draw its nutrients from the soil, but is the atmospheric equivalent of an undersea sponge, straining its moisture and nutrients from the air. It is marvellously adapted to its air-scavenging life, presenting a delicate but relatively enormous surface area in its sponge-like form. It is also marvellously efficient at holding caesium 134 and 137 and all the other radionuclides of fallout. Growing close to the ground, and only 6 centimeters tall, it intercepts 86 percent of the fallout, and holds three-quarters of it in the upper half grazed by reindeer. Only 14 percent gets into the ground, and in the absence of clays it is removed from the food chain only very slowly. The Swedes measured up to 100,000 bq/kg from the caesium 137 alone (equivalent to 150,000 with the 134 included), and the Norwegians had readings of nearly 200,000 bq. Ingested by the reindeer that first summer and autumn, the caesium moved to muscle and bone, giving readings of 4,000–24,000 bq/kg by the fall, when the biological halflife was only 5–12 days in the summer. Even in the summer, when new grass and other forage is available, the reindeer still eat lichen to supply the special bacteria in their stomachs that allow them to digest this "air sponge." But that winter, as the biological halflife rose to 18 days, and the reindeer began to rely more and more on lichen forage, the count rose rapidly to 10,000–30,000 bq. By winter's end there were readings of 50,000–80,000 bq in both Sweden and Norway, with some extremes over 100,000 bq. "We have never seen anything like this before," said one radiobiologist who had monitored the fallout from the bomb tests. And the problem is not going away: in heavily grazed areas half of the caesium is still in the lichen five years later, and in undisturbed areas the "in-the-plant-halflife" varies between eight and 14 years.

For the Sami of both countries the effect was devastating. As summer moved into autumn, and the date of the annual slaughter came closer, so both the biological halflife and the proportion of lichen in the diet rose. In one of the hardest hit areas of Norway the reindeer were cropping 3.5 kg (about 8 pounds) of lichen a day, and 80 percent was being retained in the large muscles used for meat. At the autumn slaughter in Sweden only 20 percent of the 80,000 reindeer culled were below the 300 bq limit, and most people shied away from any reindeer meat that reached the shops. An expensive marketing campaign already under way in Europe fell flat. After all the publicity few Europeans would touch the stuff. The following spring the "acceptable" level for sale was raised from 300 to 1,500 bq, but by this time it was difficult for the Sami not to take a cynical view. That first year they received compensation from the government of 100 million crowns (approximately $17 million), and many thought that the limit was raised simply to get the government off the hook. "We are told to bury all our reindeer one minute and now suddenly it's alright to eat five times the amount. What are we meant to do, dig them up?" said one herder. "It's all so senseless, killing the animals then burying them," said another. But if the roughly 35 percent are not slaughtered each year, the reindeer population will explode – the same concern expressed for the moose population – and over-grazing will result. Some meat was sold to mink farms, but it hardly made a dent in the problem. At one sale area, usually crowded with people around the corrals, only seven carcasses were for sale, and the mood of despair could be felt by the few who had bothered to turn up.

The cost has been enormous, not simply in wasted meat, but in the cost of trying to disconnect the reindeer from the lichen. "Pre-Chernobyl" or uncontaminated fodder is heavy, bulky stuff, expensive to buy and expensive to move from southern hayfields to the north. "And they really don't like it very much," said one young herder. "Their stomachs don't seem to function well on it," perhaps an astute intuitive comment on the fact that some lichen seems to be necessary to keep the special bacteria in their digestive systems going. "You can give them hay and the special food pellets they use for cows," said a herder who had spent all of his 60 years with his herds, "but the older ones won't eat." Some reindeer were trucked that winter farther south to uncontaminated pastures, but the caesium was still in the lichen when they returned the following spring.

Some attempts were made to feed reindeer with bentonite, a natural clay that has the capacity to remove the caesium by chelation. In Greek *chele* is a claw, and the molecules of bentonite literally grab the caesium and claw it out of the reindeer's system. But the same clay molecules are undiscriminating and may also eliminate valuable potassium and other nutrients. It is also an aluminum compound, and we are slowly becoming more aware of what aluminum may do to the delicate network of cells in the brain. "It may have taken out some of the caesium," said a young herder, "But the animals were all out of condition by spring and 'lazy' [I think he meant 'weak', but when a herder speaks of his reindeer you listen carefully.] We had to take them by truck to the first summer pasture because they were not strong enough to go themselves," he added. One Norwegian suggested that perhaps the reindeer were not so much "lazy" but simply out of rhythm. Taken down from the high *fjäll* much earlier than usual in an attempt to get them to less contaminated feed, the reindeer may simply have been "out of phase."

There are old rhythms here not easily broken, rhythms of nature, rhythms of the animals, and rhythms of the humans that depend upon them. "One of those scientists told us we should just change our slaughter to the summer when the reindeer are eating more grass," said one herder, "They really don't know anything, do they?" And the rhythms of nature are translated into other human rhythms too. Foods come in and out of season, berries of all sorts that are important components of Sami life and diet. Many families earn up to 50,000 crowns ($8,500) a year picking cloudberries for sale, and they put aside many for themselves. Factories preserving berries as jams, juice, and liqueurs have refused to buy fruit that tested over the limits. Fish also form an important part of the traditional diet, but in areas of peak fallout they test in many thousands of becquerels. "I've never bought a piece of fish at a store in my life," said one Sami woman, "and I'm not going to start now. We try to follow the directives from Stockholm, but our neighbors have simply given up. After all, we have to eat, and food in the shops here is expensive." As for the reindeer themselves, one Sami family will consume five to ten animals a year. Herding is an active outdoor life, often conducted in cold weather, and high calorie foods are needed. It is not the least unusual for a Sami herder and his family to have reindeer meat on the table six to eight times a week, and it forms a staple food as great slices are carved from smoked and preserved chunks of meat. An intake of a kilogram per week would be considered usual, and at 10,000 bq the arithmetic gives a dose of 47.5 mSv, nearly one hundred times the new maximum limits now recommended for "ordinary people." Only one year later the amplification effects were being measured in the radiophysics laboratory of a major northern hospital in Sweden. Non-Sami (Swedes) had whole body counts of 2,000–7,000 bq; the young Sami herders were 10,000–102,000 bq and still rising sharply. Only the caesium 137 was measured, but add in the caesium 134 and you are at 150,000 bq per 170 kg adult, and still going up. A true absorbed dose equivalent, weighing the alpha radiation as Rolf Sievert taught us to do, gives a dose of over 10 mSv. "Do you tell them and help them to understand what it means?," I asked one radiophysicist. "Well," he said "People don't behave quite the same when they know the results."

But the Sami know. Not perhaps in the cool clinical language of a medical ward, not in the abstract world of an oncologist who computes doses for things on the back of an envelope. But they know. One young herder from a peak fallout area close to Norway's border made the long overnight trip when the tests first started. "I had 8,000 becquerels back then," he said, and the look in his eyes was not something you measure. He did not return for testing. "What's the use," he said "I can't change just like that. If I move away, if I drop out, the new law says I, and all my descendants, can never take up reindeer herding again. Who do they think they are in Stockholm? We were here before there was a Stockholm. One of the bureaucrats even suggested bringing factories here to give us employment. Don't they know, don't they understand, anything?"

It is when you actually talk to the Sami that the juddering impact of this event hits you in that which makes us most truly human – language itself. In talking to Sami men and women, families who took me into their homes and showed me great kindness, I had to have some help, someone to *översätta*, to set over the Samisk into Swedish or English. Yet I listened carefully when discussions went on around me in Samisk, hoping to catch a cognate here, a clue there. Nothing. It was a human tongue decended from a line so distant and far removed from this Indo-European child that only an opaqueness of liquid sound broke over me. And then, suddenly, in the "rhubarb-rhubarb," the "bar-bar" of Samisk, the word "becquerel" exploded.

15 How to make problems disappear: The bureaucratic management of crisis

When an environmental catastrophe like Chernobyl occurs, government in many of its institutional and bureaucratic forms is immediately involved. A crisis has to be managed: that is what government is for, that is what the governed expect, and that is what those representing government attempt to do. In a modern society, of whatever political or ideological persuasion, the governed have the wholly reasonable expectation that those representing government will be competent, that the trust placed in politicians, public officials, and "experts," will be fully justified, and that an event affecting everyone will be treated openly and honestly – making some perfectly reasonable exceptions for necessary intelligence operations. Indeed a truly "modern society," as opposed to a tribal or feudal kingdom, is almost defined in terms of these expectations, presumptions expressed in laws that circumscribe the power of government to act arbitrarily and dishonestly. The ground of true governance is trust, and a government that loses the trust of the governed either does not stand, or becomes a suppressive regime controlling by force and fear, but not truly governing in the sense that the governed give their assent.

The problem with bureaucracies in the modern world is that their instincts are too frequently opposed to the openness and honesty that lead to trust. And in using a phrase like "their instincts" I am obviously not personifying bureaucracies, but only acknowledging that they are made up of many individual men and women who tend to acquire a collective attitude to the mass of people governed by the regulations of which they are the guardians, enforcers, and often the originators. Those in government bureaucracies who do not share in the collective attitude to a degree considered appropriate are simply asked to leave, or the "system" sees to it that they never reach positions where their views have much chance of making an impact. Whistle blowers are particularly not appreciated, and everything is done to remove them from the system as soon as possible – as the American space and Star Wars programs

demonstrate so vividly and so often. One of America's most distinguished health physicists, a man labelled by one atomic energy commis-
sioner as "one of the best occupational epidemiologists in the world,"
was fired by the Atomic Energy Commission when he wanted to publish
his careful analysis of the Hanford plant in Washington state, and his data
were confiscated. Two years later a congressional subcommittee decided
that he had been dismissed as a calculated attempt to hide his findings.

It is important that the game is played properly even as the boat is not
rocked. Paradoxically, bureaucrats fully expect the trust of the governed,
and if cynicism has not set in they are hurt or outraged in the face of any
expressions of doubt. At the same time they tend to grow increasingly
distrustful of the governed, and oppose strongly anything of genuine
democratic form like a "Freedom of Information Act." After a while the
governed tend to become "them," and therefore not "us," and since
"they" are the ones being governed it means, almost by definition, that
they are not really fit to take part in the permanent bureaucratic
structures of government. Anyway "they" cannot really understand the
issues and difficulties, and could not interpret the information properly
even if they had it. That is why we have civil services, armed forces, and a
host of permanent government experts and employees who are not
subject to the stress of elections – unlike the politicians who come and go
on the whims of these popularity polls.

If, as a bureaucrat, you have confidence in the collective wisdom and
ability of those around you, you have essentially seven ways to deal with
an environmental crisis of some magnitude – apart from being open and
honest about it, including admitting you do not know the answer to a
particular question but are doing your best to find out. In general terms
these are: suppression or covering up; defining the problem away;
authoritative belittling; arithmetic obfuscation; public relations; creative
deception; and information reduction. All seven of these tactics were
employed instinctively by bureaucracies in both eastern and western
Europe, but probably most creatively and effectively in the practiced
hands of the British and French, two governments employing the bastion
of freedom and the revolutionary inheritance images respectively to
demonstrate how democratic they are. Both have civil services whose
senior members have vigorously and successfully opposed anything
approaching a Freedom of Information Act. In Britain today the
bureaucratic instinct to keep public information away from the public is
strongly supported by a government whose members have successfully
defeated every attempt to rescind an Act allowing the suppression of
publications "in the national interest." The Act was passed during a
period of public hysteria over spies in 1915, and has provided the legal

means for the D-notice ever since, making editors personally punishable by heavy jail sentences if they publish any material that senior civil servants or politicians consider embarrassing. For example, only in 1988 did the story of the graphite fire of 1957 at Windscale come out. It was then learnt that all the senior scientists of the time had urged immediate publication, but the reports were suppressed by the Prime Minister himself (Harold Macmillan), presumably in a national interest that was not considered congruent with a truth that could save human lives in the future. In France other controls are available, but they are just as effective.

It is important to state this forthrightly because managing an atomic crisis requires that governments bring into the advisory circle those whom they consider to have the greatest expertise. In general, this means that atomic physicists and atomic engineers in the atomic power industry provide most of the advice about an atomic crisis. In brief, important and direct advisory channels open up to those with the greatest personal stake in atomic energy. In other areas of government, suspicions of conflict of interest might be aroused, but scientists of either the pure or applied variety are known to be objective seekers after the truth. To think that their scientific judgements might be swayed in any way by personal predilection or career considerations would be uncharitable at best and slanderous at worst. In fact, any expressions of doubt about the objective veracity of scientists might well be suppressed themselves, for obviously these could not be rational, and there is no reason why a society founded on reason should publish the ravings of the irrational. We have other ways of helping such people, because psychiatry is quite advanced these days. We obviously ask atomic scientists about atomic power and, if it does not embarrass them too much, about atomic mishaps whose probability has been scientifically computed by the scientists to be so low that for all practical purposes there cannot possibly be any cause for alarm. We trust scientists, and we must trust them, because they are the experts in these technically complex areas which ordinary people cannot possibly understand. Hence these distressingly emotional outbursts by lay people who react simply out of ignorance.

During the Chernobyl crisis a great deal of information was manipulated or suppressed by governments advised by atomic scientists and engineers. During the research for this book, research covering 5,000–6,000 pages of official reports, eyewitness statements, scientific treatises, and media accounts, I formed, recorded, evaluated, and carefully revised impressions of the degree to which governments had engaged in suppressive tactics to deal with the management problem facing them. These "impressions" will immediately be dismissed by some as biased, but I have made every effort to make as fair and as accurate judgements as I can. "Suppression" may be a difficult thing to measure with scientific precision, but you recognize it when you see it, and you can certainly order it from "low" to "high." For example, I came across no attempt whatsoever to suppress information in Norway, but a number of very strong pieces of evidence that suppression was distressingly high in Poland.

There is no question in my own mind that there was a direct and strong correlation between the degree to which a country had made itself dependent on atomic power and the degree to which it employed the tactic of suppressing information (figure 5). This is only an attempt to formalize and make reasonably well defined a view widely expressed, and it is hardly an original finding on my part. A number of people have expressed the same thing, and one large European consumer group noted "It is significant that those countries with the highest dependency on nuclear power tended to do the least [in the way of providing information], with the obvious exception of Germany."

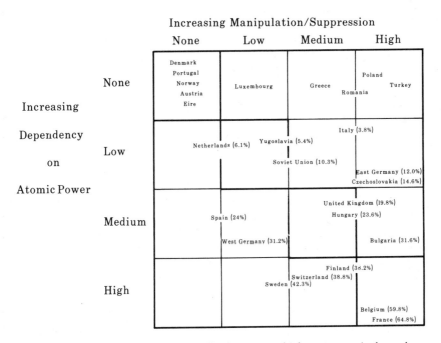

Figure 5 The relationship between the degree to which a country is dependent on atomic power, and the degree to which information about Chernobyl's effects were manipulated or suppressed.

Exceptions to rules are important, and you obviously have to have a rule before you can have an exception to it. What is the rule? If it were perfect, all the countries would lie in those diagonal boxes from Eire and her four non-atomic companions in the top lefthand corner, to Belgium and France, well over 60 percent dependent, in the bottom righthand corner. The rule would say that more atomic power inevitably brings more information suppression in its wake. But it is not a perfect rule, and some of the exceptions are easy to explain. Most of those in the top righthand corner are eastern European countries whose governments already exert a high degree of control over the dissemination of information, and who have built, or are committed to building, Soviet designed atomic reactors. It is highly embarrassing to wake up one morning to find the main designer and supplier of your reactors, not to say your ideological compatriot, dealing with a catastrophe that is dumping very heavy radioactivity on you. Your instinct is to suppress as much information as you can, and hope that the problem will go away. Greece and Turkey, even without atomic power of their own, exerted a fairly heavy hand, suppressing information about the high levels of fallout for political and economic reasons respectively.

On the other side of the diagonal – rather less suppression than we would expect from our rule – we find Spain with nearly a quarter of her electricity produced by atomic power, but virtually untouched by the fallout herself. The accident affecting much of the rest of Europe was fully reported, although it was made clear that such an event could not possibly happen in Spain itself and there was no cause for alarm. Politically, Finland finds itself in a delicate "in-between" position, and it has not always been easy for antinuclear groups to get full and accurate information. The Finns are also very circumspect about broadcasting unfavorable news about the Soviet Union, especially when it is picked up on Estonian television across the Gulf. Nevertheless, pressure from the media produced somewhat less suppression than we might expect. Switzerland is in the same box for a different reason. One acquires a rather strong impression of a government doing very little, rather than actively suppressing information. Sweden is a more complex case, generally very open despite the high dependence on atomic power, but with some subtle and disturbing currents underneath the surface.

Finally, West Germany, strongly committed to atomic power, was extraordinarily open thanks to strong local powers and political pressures brought to bear by the Green Party. One gets the impression that bureaucrats in the Federal government found it difficult to manipulate information because of a marked capacity to generate sound scientific information at the regional level. If you want to suppress information you must keep a tight control from the center and allow as little local autonomy as possible. Despite a traditional tendency towards rigid bureaucracy and "the correct way of doing things," West Germany showed what a vigorous federal structure could achieve. There is little point in suppressing information in Bavaria if the local newspapers are full of it next door. And if university scientists at Konstanz insist on doing their measurements, then the bureaucrats of Stuttgart might as well join them because they obviously cannot beat them.

Suppressing information was not the only tactic employed. Sometimes facts come out that have to be dealt with bureaucratically in other ways. One is to define the problem away. Yesterday 300 bq/kg defined the limit above which your responsible government could not possibly allow food to enter the market and food chain. Today it is 1,500 bq so we really do not have much of a problem anymore. As it was put so nicely in the innocuous accounting language of thrift, "People have to establish their own becquerel budgets." Probably not more than 50,000 bq a year, unless unusual "cultural circumstances" arise, at which point you might consider 500,000 bq. Thus today's "spokesmen" for Sweden's National Institute of Radiation Protection do a Pontius Pilate act while pointing at the same time to the Sami – a feat of considerable manual dexterity. The redefinition tactic also tends to be employed in direct proportion to the dependence on atomic power. Britain and France press for a 5,000 bq limit on foodstuffs, and claim in an international forum that "This is the only scientific proposal before us," even as Denmark is asking for the current limit of 600 bq to be lowered even further on the grounds of what heavy alpha particles can do to living tissue.

Another way to manage the problem is to get an authority figure to belittle the numbers and the concern they generate. A director of a national laboratory, for example, notes that the probability of one of our reactors having an accident is "extremely small;" another points out that the fallout is only three or four times the background, as if this were nothing to worry about; a noted radiologist, used to thinking about beta and gamma energies used in hospital X-rays and treatments, reports in his familiar grays and forgets that Rolf Sievert taught him to weight the alpha radiation by a factor of 20. In most hospital applications alpha particles are properly ignored, but when caesium is in the food chain they should not be "forgotten" and left out. A physicist notes that "a dose of 43 rems does less damage than a lifetime of cigarette smoking," a criterion that may not have been the most wisely chosen.

A further "authority" tactic is to put out seemingly altruistic "information" for the general public which is simply dissimulating and deceitful propaganda. Two years after Chernobyl, one of the major groups of the atomic energy industry in the United States put out a "trashing piece" to show that Chernobyl's fallout posed no hazard whatsoever. It drew entirely on newspaper articles, and one or two reports of the Swedish atomic energy industry, which was also trying to minimize the dangers. It then listed many articles from genuine scientific journals to give the appearance of scientific veracity, but a careful reader could easily see that none of these referred to any Chernobyl or post-Chernobyl effects. All reported on pre-Chernobyl matters, some relating to atomic bomb testing in the 1960s!

The management of such a large scale environmental problem also provides many opportunities for creative deception, including the venting of radioactive gases from underground bomb tests in Nevada when minute amounts of Chernobyl fallout finally reach Chicago lying in the direct path of the winds. This same tactic can also employ arithmetic obfuscation, averaging high peaks away with low regional values to produce no cause for alarm. Indeed, the enthusiasm with which these tactics are employed may lead to some puzzling contradictions. As one British scientific journal noted "The oddity of an official position which claims that deaths can be caused by an episode which poses 'no health risk' has never been explained."

Finally, if you want a problem to go away, it is important not to do anything that would allow pertinent data to be accumulated in a form either accessible to the public or generally pertinent to a scientific analysis. Both international commissions and individual scientists in the weeks following Chernobyl recommended what a geographer would call a Geographical Information System (GIS), a computerized data bank into which every scrap of information, every test, every reading across Europe, would be stored with its (x, y, t) – its latitude, longitude and time – coordinates. One scientist, with a lifetime in medical physics, noted "It is regrettable that society is not set up to provide such information on a timely basis. However, if the will exists to obtain such data the opportunity has not been lost."

But despite recommendations from commissions and knowledgeable specialists, the opportunity has been lost, both on a national and international basis. The technical capability is certainly there. Compared to the data handling capacities used routinely in remote sensing today, even in undergraduate geography courses, the data bank requirements are trivial in size and cost. But the will does not exist to record, collate, and analyse the data to reach a deeper and longer-term understanding. Yet only by recording the data in their specific time and space coordinates could we ever make reasonable estimates of the numbers of people who will die of cancers, or those who will have to bear the trauma of malignancies that are labelled non-fatal, but whose psychic burden and anguish are not measured by becquerels. With sufficiently fine-grained geographic data we could make some genuinely reasonable estimates. Unfortunately, there is no will, and perhaps many of those "managing" the crisis would prefer that the signal is so conveniently lost in the noise. But despite the way governments have tried to manage the crisis, the anxiety will not go away. Trust in science and government has taken a very heavy blow. The caesium is transmitted on the food chains, and all the other connections and structures of the natural world, and moves over to the political, economic, and social structures of the human world. There it has the effect of dissolving the glue of trust that holds these structures together. Nowhere is this seen more clearly than in the changing attitudes towards atomic power. It is time we looked at these explicitly.

16   Cost and safety: A very silly way to boil water

In the early 1970s, with the tide in favor of nuclear power running at full flood, Austria's government decided not to be left behind in the enthusiastic scramble towards the new atomic age. All the large and powerful countries had already committed themselves, and the technology was so well known and well tested that you could compute the minute probabilities of failure. These were so small that it would be an unseemly and backward response if one failed to move towards those brightly lit uplands of the future, uplands of civilized life lit by cheap and unlimited atomic power. True, a referendum had been promised by the Socialist Party "before the final decision is made," but construction began anyway because the outcome of the referendum was surely obvious, and it only represented a token bone thrown to the emotional trouble makers. After all, the people of Austria were a sensible and sober lot, and would realize that government experts had taken advice in a highly technical area from scientific experts who had studied such specialized things in the university.

In 1979, the year of Three Mile Island (TMI), the promised referendum was held. The sensible and sober people of Austria turned down atomic power flat, and the boiling water reactors of Zwentendorf were mothballed. Like their bureaucratic peers in Stockholm, many in Vienna have been casting around ever since looking for some plausible excuse to hold another referendum to reverse the first. After all, TMI got a lot of publicity but it really was not that bad; no other accidents had occurred; and in the long run you could even say TMI was a good thing because all sorts of even more reliable safety procedures could now be put in place. But even that sort of thinking changed with Chernobyl. In the Austrian presidential campaigns both the Conservative and Socialist candidates declared they were for dismantling Zwentendorf, and the Chancellor announced "The use of atomic energy in Austria can be considered closed." It was, ran the general opinion, a very silly way to boil water.

TMI started the process of rethinking all over the world, confirming the doubts a few had, and making others who had not thought about it very much worried and anxious. Where a national expression was possible, the Swedes said "none after 2010," and the Austrians said "no ... period." Where referenda were not available, unofficial public opinion polls said the same thing. All over the Western world, small groups protested around atomic plants, but many of the participants had long hair, funny beads, and rumpled clothes, and probably smoked marijuana as well. Most people thought there must be a better way to express their anxiety (80 percent of Americans now disapprove of atomic power), but what could the individual really do to fight City Hall when City Hall consisted of an industry worth hundreds of billions, an industry coddled and pampered by successive governments on a scale never seen before in human history? The connections between money and political power were so tight it was sometimes difficult to see the seams where they joined. In many European countries, where the atomic power industry was nationalized or partially owned by the state, atomic energy was part of government and there were no seams to see.

TMI started it, but human memories are short and impressionable. Hundreds of millions of dollars were invested in public relations and advertising by the atomic power industry and its government agencies to make sure the impressions were favorable. Since Chernobyl the reaction has been the same. You let the antinuclear "crackpots" have their say, give them enough rope to hang themselves with obviously absurd and emotional statements that can be demolished on scientific grounds, and then you reach for the fat PR wallet. Two tightly intertwined issues are involved – cost and safety – but no amount of PR money seems to be able to dispose of the facts that lie just beneath the surface of these most visible concerns.

In the 1960s, atomic power promised the cleanest, cheapest, most abundant source of energy the world had ever seen. Not only could enormous profits be made, but it was environmentally responsible too. No acid rain, no polluted streams, no more beautiful habitats gouged by huge shovels – atomic power would open up a new age of peace and prosperity. Everyone knew that world tensions were created by shortages of resources, the most important of which was energy. Solve this problem and recycling would take care of the rest. Out of the ashes of death and destruction in war would come the phoenix of peace. For those who had committed themselves in wartime to the forces of light against the forces of darkness, atomic power promised justification and redemption after the horror and revulsion of Hiroshima and Nagasaki.

In the United States, the leading atomic nation, the land of free enterprise and government-assisted competition, the early years of the atomic power industry were like the early days of the automobile.

Everyone jumped into the act offering variation this, improvement that, with the result that cost effective standardization and economies of scale went by the board. Not that it mattered much. The atomic power industry was the most protected industry the world had ever seen, its research and development supported by a cozy relationship with the government that supplied the huge funds that bought the brightest scientific and engineering talents. There were virtually no economic penalties for mistakes, and firms supplying most of the equipment were the same firms supplying many of America's defense needs. In both these strongly related areas the sky of cost overruns is the limit: the American taxpayer and consumer will always cough up more. In many respects the industry was driven by the Atomic Energy Commission (AEC) itself, particularly after an aggressive Wall Street banker was appointed as its head and took it into the public domain with a snowstorm of pamphlets and television announcements in ten languages around the world.

The earliest civilian plant was a joint effort between Westinghouse and the Duquesne Light Company of Pittsburgh, blessed by the trinity of the AEC, the US Navy, and the President of the United States. Other power companies were cautious at first, in spite of $1.3 billion spent by the AEC in promoting civilian power. After all, if the Navy could live under the arctic ice for months at a time in an atomic submarine, what had the civilian population to fear? Then General Electric made an unprecedented offer, a fixed price contract to Jersey Central Light and Power in 1963 for a plant on Oyster Creek. It was this initial, highly subsidized "showpiece" that broke through the doubts and hesitations. Three years later, 30 reactors were on order, although most of them had already changed to cost-plus contracts, for the early plants had lost the makers roughly $75 million each. Cost-plus contracts simply absolved the makers of any risk and put the total cost on the power companies, who thought they would simply shift the cost to the consumers.

These costs have been staggering. In 1970, when roughly 80 atomic plants were on order or already building, a plant cost about $125 for each kilowatt hour it could produce. It doubled to $250 four years later, doubled again to $500 by 1978, doubled again to $1,000 by 1982, doubled to $2,000 four years later, and is right on target for doubling again to $4,000 by 1990. Seabrook in New Hampshire went from $1.0 billion to $4.5 billion in the 11 years it was building, and early in 1988 Public Service of New Hampshire filed for bankruptcy. Diablo Canyon in California cost an order of magnitude (ten times) more, going from $450 million to $4.4 billion, and a plant in Indiana nearly doubled its cost from $1.4 billion to $2.5 billion, only to give up completely when it was only half finished. Average costs of atomic power are now twice those from other sources. During 1980, 54 plants were cancelled (108 since 1974), and no new orders have been made. For all practical purposes there is a moratorium on atomic power in America. One hard headed business magazine wrote "The failure of the US nuclear power program ranks as the largest managerial disaster in business history, a disaster on monumental scale."

Elsewhere the stories are mostly variations on this theme, although costs in nationalized industries are more difficult to estimate and easier to hide. A gas cooled reactor at Dungeness in Britain went from $160 million to $1.1 billion, and none of the 18 water reactors planned in 1974 has been built. Abandoned plants litter the atomic landscapes of Europe, Asia and the Americas – Yugoslavia, Spain, China, Mexico, Brazil, Argentina to name just a few – and France now has an excess of capacity and more troubles than she cares to admit, ranging from accidents that are covered up to huge debts that are skillfully hidden in national accounts. Even the Soviet Union has reported so much opposition to new construction at Krasnodar (southeast of Chernobyl) that the atomic plant has been cancelled.

But cost is not really the main reason for anxiety, particularly where the state owns the power generating facilities and can easily subsidize costs with a mixture of outright grants and "creative accounting." For the general public, for governments informed ultimately by public opinion, and even among people in the atomic energy industry itself, the major doubt is the question of safety. Here the litany of accidents makes truly grim reading, and the mood is translated into both collective decision and individual concern. Utility stocks are fairly stable, even stolid investments, but if the stock market really reflects astute financial opinion, then the collective judgement of investors has decided against atomic power, hammering the stocks of many utility companies generating this form of energy. As for the insurance industry, it decided long ago that it would not insure against nuclear accident at any price or premium. Even most personal insurances – homes, automobiles, etc – are not liable today for any damage caused by a nuclear accident. Take a look at your fine print. In 1956, a study commission by the AEC on the effects of a "maximum credible accident" estimated 3,400 deaths and 43,000 injured. The result was the Price–Anderson Act of 1957, limiting the liability of the power companies to $560 million dollars, with $500 million coming from the taxpayer. An update of the AEC study in 1964 showed that 45,000 would be killed and 100,000 injured, with a price tag of $50 billion (late 1980s prices) in property damage. The US Congress has extended and revised the Price–Anderson Act several times, and in 1988, by an overwhelming majority, raised the liability on the nuclear industry from $710 million to

$7.1 billion before the taxpayer would shoulder the rest. Even so, what price would you care to put on your son and daughter, your wife, your grandmother . . . ? All these reports were extremely embarrassing to the AEC, and would probably have been suppressed but for the threat of a suit in 1973. They were certainly enough to make one of America's most lucrative industries, the insurance business, reflect upon its responsibilities to its shareholders.

But the greatest concern rises from the frequency of accidents themselves, and it may only now be slowly dawning that in those early and heavily subsidized "jump in and shake out" days of the industry the most ill-advised, perhaps catastrophic, decision was made when the light water reactor was almost universally adopted as the basic type of design. It is what one atomic engineer has called "an exceedingly complex and unforgiving device." Because it was designed initially under defense pressure and funding for submarine propulsion, it just "happened to be available" when the drive from atoms-for-war to atoms-for-peace was started. While the many light water designs differ in important ways, we know essentially how they work: ordinary water is used both as a moderator and as a coolant. Providing you have a reactor with a negative void coefficient, loss of water as a moderator is fine. Everything slows down and finally shuts off. But loss of water as a coolant is a disaster, and much of the increased cost in building light water reactors comes down to providing backup systems of backup systems of backup systems, a chain of purposeful, built in redundancy that is termed "defense in depth." But the result is perhaps an even greater nightmare of complexity.

In a graphite moderated reactor, a thousand or more tubes penetrate the core and join in a mare's nest of pipes, joints and couplings at top and bottom, any one of which could corrode and fail under the intense heat and pressure, and so lead to local overheating and fracturing of the fuel tubes. It is a nice question how you conduct "local repairs" on an atomic reactor when you must force cooling water through under high pressure and dare not shut it off for fear of making things worse. Both Hanford, Washington, and Savannah River, South Carolina, are graphite moderated and have a long history of accidents, starting in 1949 when Hanford released 2×10^{16} becquerels into the atmosphere, roughly 20 times TMI. As Hanford has aged so the accidents have increased, releasing another 2×10^{16} becquerels over its lifetime. It was shut down six times in 1986, and one of the incidents was so severe it could have led to an uncontrolled chain reaction. Nine kilograms of plutonium were also missing, either "stuck in the pipes somewhere" said a spokesman, "or an illusion due to inconsistencies in accounting." In 1987 it was closed down for repairs for an indefinite time and Savannah River followed. In Britain, a reprocessing plant also "lost" 25 kilograms of plutonium in the tubes, and only very narrowly averted a chain reaction when more plutonium was put in the system.

In light water reactors, using water as the moderator, the accident record is no better. In 1985 alone there were nearly 3,000 reportable accidents in American reactors, and while some may have been quite trivial, the 764 emergency shutdowns were just that – shutdowns under genuine emergency conditions that often produce great reactor stress due to the intense heat and pressures involved. A study by the US government noted that in the decade 1969–79 there were 169 incidents that could have led to meltdown conditions. At one reactor a pipe was plugged by wrapping a basketball in tape, but pressure built up and blew the ball like a bullet from the pipe releasing 14,000 gallons of radioactive water. Safety tests have not been conducted, safety equipment has been installed upside down or backwards, and in one plant an entire set of welding equipment was eventually found in a pipe carrying cooling water. At another, a drinking fountain was inadvertently connected to a tank for radioactive waste, an incident that was labelled "poor practice." Often conditions were so faulty that operators no longer trusted the instruments that were meant to give them reliable information. It is rather like a pilot flying in mountainous terrain saying "I'll try to see through the fog because the altimeter's probably no good tonight."

Sometimes things get so bad that even the atomic industry itself turns on one of its own. In March 1986, the US Nuclear Regulatory Commission (NRC) ordered the Peach Bottom nuclear plant of Philadelphia Electric, about 45 miles south of TMI, to shut down after operators in the control room were found asleep on the job. They were unable to stand hours of watching hundreds of dials, and many were in the habit of reading or falling asleep instead. The practices at Peach Bottom had been known for years in the industry itself, and the Institute of Nuclear Power Operations (INPO), an industry watchdog set up after TMI, had written numerous letters with such phrases as "a substantial upgrade is necessary," "unacceptable pattern of performance," and "an embarrassment to the industry and nation." With nearly a million people within an 80 km (50 mile) radius, they had reason to be worried. Eventually the president of the company resigned, and the plant was shut down for over three years.

All of the mishaps involve interactions between the human being and the machine, and in the face of such complexity, with so much information arriving to be assimilated and acted upon, it is really not surprising that nearly all accidents have involved human error. It is here that we meet what we might call the dilemma of the "Cascading Apprentice." As the reactor operators, the apprentices to the sorcerer, attempt to control the complexity they often make things worse, producing a cascade of errors, each of which may be small but amplifies the initial problem steadily towards catastrophe. TMI, for example, started when a small amount of water inadvertently entered an air line and stopped a pump, at which point the operators did not have enough information to take the correct action. As one scientific journal noted in a gallant effort to cut through obfuscating language reflecting equally obfuscating thinking: "[It doesn't do much good blaming things] on a 'faulty mental model' . . . This seems to complicate the issue needlessly. The notion of a mental model is redundant – at best a metaphor. To have an accurate model is to know what is going on; to have a faulty mental model is not to know . . . the operators of TMI [did not know] what was going on when they made their fatal errors." In other words, when something highly complex goes wrong, you need the right information to decide upon lines of action that have been designed beforehand to meet every possible contingency.

Finding out what is wrong with a light water reactor is just one example of the general field of diagnostics, something we are all familiar with, whether we are feeling ill and wondering how to get better, or simply trying to figure out why the car will not start this morning. All are specific examples of abstract "problem solving," a general area of knowledge with lots of formal mathematical analyses and proofs of theorems, most of which boil down to the perfectly commonsensical idea that the more things you connect up into a big system, the more difficult that big system is going to be to control. One answer, some say, is to recognize that only machines can control machines, which means essentially that only computers can sift through enormous amounts of information, find the right "diagnostic combination," and take action with electric signals to make the mechanical levers work. In Britain a new light water reactor built to work at extremely high pressures, has automatic controls deliberately designed to make it very difficult for a human operator to interfere for the first 30 minutes after an accident. The human beings just stand there and watch the machines. But this "solution" raises more problems. First, any accident that the computer might deal with must be an accident the designers could conceive happening before the reactor went into operation. Unfortunately, the accidents that seem to cause most of the cascades are those nobody thought would happen, what one psychologist called "unexpected and nasty surprises." Surprises are answers to questions that have not been asked. Secondly, you have to have flawless computer software, tens of thousands of lines of computer code that are without "bugs." But now another problem comes up: testing and maintaining not only the complex mechanical systems themselves, but also the computer programs that will run and control them, often "sabotages" the systems by injecting flaws into a rather delicate, almost symbiotic relationship between the two. A welder leaves his goggles in a pipe; one IF statement in half a million lines of computer code sends the diagnostic loop to the wrong button. In Britain, where software design tends to be more advanced than in the United States, specifications state that the software should not fail more than once in 100 million reactor years. But one expert noted, "these are orders of magnitude beyond what we can guarantee scientifically . . . and nobody is collecting statistically valid data on the types of faults that can occur." Even the Nuclear Installations Inspectorate said "this probabilistic approach is not the right way," and in essence condemned all the hocus-pocus of calculating probabilities out of thin air and even thinner assumptions. "Never mind," say the AI (Artificial Intelligence) specialists, "there's really no need to worry any more. We can write programs that will not only control, but also learn from their mistakes." The problem is that mistakes in atomic energy can be expensive, and the accidents an AI program might learn from are unlikely to leave much of the AI program around to do the learning.

In designing safety through the "defense in depth" principle, the last line of defense is the containment building. If the worst comes to the worst with meltdowns, and steam and hydrogen explosions, at least the radioactivity and debris will be locked up in a "containment structure." Immediately after Chernobyl a number of people in the atomic energy industries of the West made highly critical remarks about the "lack of a containment building," and went on to reassure everyone that "it couldn't possibly happen here." Both lines of criticism were misleading at best. Reactor 4 at Chernobyl was not encased in some flimsy structure that just fell apart, but was one massively strong structure inside another. The reactor casing itself had a floor and wall of steel reinforced concrete 2 meters (6 1/2 feet) thick, with a "biological shield" cap 3 meters (10 feet) thick weighing a thousand tons. All of this was encased in the reactor hall with outer walls of reinforced concrete 1.5 meters (5 feet) thick and a roof supported by steel trusses 6 meters (20 feet) deep. The steam–hydrogen explosion blew it to smithereens, but no one can say it was jerry built.

The rather condescending finger-pointing immediately after Chernobyl soon turned to a rather uncomfortable self-examination. Blowing apart two layers of reinforced concrete 11 feet thick brought a tinge of anxiety to the most blasé engineer, and America's NRC decided to look for a few motes in their own eyes before pointing to beams in the Soviets'. By December 1986, the survey concluded that a quarter of the fabled "fail-safe" containment buildings were suspect, and that the containment design "is thought by our staff to have a high likelihood of failure during a core meltdown accident." In Britain, despite reassurances by certain industrial "lordships," it was learnt that reactor containment buildings were similar to Chernobyl's, and even the French admitted they were modifying their containment designs. As well they might: Germany's containment structures are designed to withstand the impact of a jet fighter traveling at 0.6 Mach (very roughly 800 kilometers or 500 miles per hour). Most French containment buildings would not withstand the impact of a light plane.

The possibility of a plane crashing into an atomic plant seems remote, but in a world of suicidal terrorists prepared to blow themselves up with trucks loaded with explosives the chance of such a deliberate terrorist attack has made one highly influential proponent of nuclear energy change his mind. One distinguished physicist and philosopher (the brother of West Germany's president), had supported nuclear energy since 1957 as a director of a Max Planck Institute and as an advisor on national security policy. He changed his mind a year before Chernobyl because of "sleepless nights" worrying about how nuclear power plants could be protected against terrorist attacks. The issue becomes even more critical now that France has loaded her reactors with highly dangerous plutonium 239, the first time this step has been taken in a commercially operating reactor. She also has severe leakage problems, as her Superphenix is "dribbling" the liquid sodium used to cool the core, and it is difficult to find such leaks. Sodium bursts into flame when it touches water, as every high school chemistry student knows who has watched the rather dramatic demonstration with a small amount of the soft metal dropped into a basin of water. Sodium fires in fast-breeder reactors are not uncommon, and all have suffered boiler and corrosion problems because materials under constant neutron bombardment become brittle and more liable to failure. Add a containment building that could not even stop a faintly determined Piper Cub and you have a scenario for disaster.

Wherever a country has opted for atomic power, the accident story is repeated again and again as variations on a too-familiar theme. Yugoslavia shut down its American built reactor at Krsko indefinitely after facing 36 emergency shutdowns in six years; France has had several serious accidents which only became known years later, Czechoslovakia admitted to 15 defects in her plants in 1986 alone; even Sweden had to close its Barsebäck plant for 22 weeks in 1979 when corroded turbine blades caused a fire. Corrosion also caused leaks at Ringhals, and corrosion becomes an increasingly difficult problem all over the world as power plants age. Few materials can stand up to intense radioactive bombardment, and metals lose their carefully designed capabilities and specifications.

Unfortunately, the problems of safety in the nuclear power industry do not stop at the gates. Two further and very serious safety problems emerge. First, there is strong evidence that childhood leukemias cluster around major atomic facilities, particularly those reprocessing nuclear fuels, or making plutonium or other radionuclides for bombs and their triggers. In Britain, Windscale–Sellafield has become notorious for its discharges into the environment, and along with Harwell, Culham and Aldermaston in England, and Dounray, Chapelcross and Hunterston in Scotland, it has clusters of leukemias and other forms of cancer – cervical, prostate, testicular – around it. After a searing and highly controversial television program highlighted the long-suspected clusters around Sellafield, the British government appointed an investigating committee which eventually published the Black Report. This brought the Scottish verdict of "not proven," but this was widely interpreted as a noncommittal device by a government committee to protect a government installation producing three-quarters of all of Europe's atomic pollution. The European Parliament has voted to close Sellafield down – much to the embarrassment of Britain's government, which resolutely ignored the vote and refused to implement it.

The problem with "clusters" of leukemias is that it used to be difficult to demonstrate that they were caused by something in the immediate environment. If you draw pairs of random numbers as coordinates on a map, and plot the points, you will always produce some clusters just by chance. "See," say the statisticians employed by the nuclear power industry. "You have nothing but a chance effect." But when "chance clusters" cluster around atomic facilities notorious for their discharges you do not have to throw your commonsense out of the window no matter what the statisticians say. Secondly, to say that a particular cluster on the map is significant, means that you can say that is three, four, five . . . times "above the national average." But these measures are always "so many leukemias per so many people in a certain area," and depending on the area you choose you can get almost any result you like. Take a small area, and the density of leukemias is far above the national average; take a large area and the leukemia density is about the national average; take an even larger area, perhaps neatly gerrymandered to include moorland where no one lives, and your cluster is far below the national average, pointing to a fine and healthy place to live.

Fortunately, a British geographer, using a large and fast computer, has solved this problem now by examining very systematically the cluster question at all conceivable and relevant geographic scales. In the north of England, for example, the computer looked at 9 million possibilities, and each time it found a cluster at a certain scale, and at a rather stringent level of significance, it automatically plotted the circle it had used on a map. At the end of the analysis, Sellafield was a massive black blob, indicating leukemia clustering at so many different scales that it made it very difficult for even government statisticians to denigrate the results. In contrast, when the geographer's Geographical Analytical Machine (GAM) was let loose on a cancer that was known to have a purely genetic cause, and so might be expected to occur at random, no black blobs appeared.

The second problem lying "beyond the gates" is the problem of waste disposal. Ideally we would like to shoot all the highly radioactive waste from atomic plants into space or into the sun, but given a lack of reliable catapults we dare not risk a rocket carrying a radioactive payload falling back to earth, or perhaps exploding because the O-rings are a bit chilly this morning. Another solution would be to bury the wastes so deeply that they would eventually be carried down into the subduction zones where the great plates of the earth meet in tectonic collision. The problem is how to get down there.

The "solution" to the waste disposal problem so far has been to store the concentrated discharges in tanks or drums and hope that someone will come up with something in the future, or simply try to discharge the waste into the environment when no one is looking. Between 1949 and 1977 the British dumped 147 kilograms of plutonium from its atomic energy industry into the Irish Sea, and between 1968 and 1979 Sellafield alone discharged 180 kilograms more. In 1974 Sellafield had 1.8×10^{16} (18 quadrillion) becquerels in liquid-slurry storage, about half the entire discharge from Chernobyl, and did not know what to do with it. The managing director of British Nuclear Fuels pooh-poohed the discharges (now dumped straight from the hulls of specially designed ships to avoid unpleasant confrontations with Greenpeace when dumping over the side), and noted that 10,000 tons of uranium occurred quite naturally "on the sea bed" of the Irish Sea, so what was a few hundred kilograms more? But his definition of "sea bed" had to go 200 meters down into the silts and bedrock to accumulate that 10,000 tons, and the 100 square kilometers (a radius of about 6 kilometers from the discharge pipe), contained only 25 kilograms naturally in the top 10 centimeters of the sea floor affecting living sea creatures. So an extra discharge of 400 kilograms of plutonium will have a marked effect, and will keep on having an effect for the next quarter of a million years.

The same problems face every country that has moved into atomic power without thinking the matter of waste disposal through. There is a frantic hunt for sites that are "safe," but we are talking about dumps that may be radioactive for half a million years. Two physicists noted that the search for a waste site in the United States "has been abused at every turn ... The Department of Energy has lost all credibility." The very government department responsible for producing the largest amount of atomic waste in the world has been charged with finding a suitable dumping site. It is difficult to find a more blatant case of conflict of interest. Meanwhile handling waste today produces highly dangerous conditions. Even ignoring the leakage of waste into the Columbia River and ground water, a Hanford practice of pouring relatively low-level waste into unlined trenches eventually produced a more and more concentrated layer of plutonium in the soil. Fortunately, it was removed by the AEC in time, but it could have created a chain reaction if heavy rain had suddenly moderated the neutron flux. It is strongly suspected today that a disastrous atomic accident at Kyshtym in the Soviet Union during December–January 1957–8 was due to an explosion in a nuclear waste dump.

Some have suggested that atomic waste could be incorporated into highly stable borosilicate glasses and artificial "rocks" so chemically stable that they could be buried or dumped safely at sea. The costs of such processing are unknown at the moment, but are probably five to ten times higher than estimated if the past is any sort of guide to the future. These costs will send the kilowatt hour costs of atomic power doubling into the future as they have been doubling since 1970.

A final problem of cost and safety is one that will have to be faced very soon as older plants come to the end of their useful commercial lifetimes, or as decisions are made to close down plants because they are unsafe or uneconomic. It is the problem of decommissioning, of somehow closing down the plant for good and dismantling it, rather than building a massive sarcophagus around it. Nobody knows very much about taking an atomic plant apart safely, but TMI and Chernobyl point to some of the difficulties ahead. First, the cost may be very large, although for the moment it is rather desperately being minimized by an industry hoping the decommissioning problems will somehow be solved by the time they come up. Even so, estimates for Sellafield's gas cooled reactor, and the same sort of reactor at Chinon in France, run at around $200 per kilowatt. For a reactor in the 1,000 megawatt range this means $150 million, but many think this is going to prove absurdly low. The decommissioning and decontamination of TMI has proved much more difficult and expensive than originally thought, with the cost mounting to $1 billion over seven years. The Shoreham reactor in New York State will take $5.3 billion to tear down, and no one is quite sure how to approach and dispose of the radioactive core. Simply to clean up the Hanford, Washington, and the Savannah River, South Carolina, weapons plants will cost $50 billion over 30 years, and a US Senate subcommittee was highly skeptical that this would be sufficient. Similarly, in Britain, $500 million has been set aside to decommission the Berkeley reactor, but few believe that this will be close to the final costs.

Cost and safety: on the evidence one is very high, the other very low. But men have staked their professional lives and reputations on what has been built so far, and find it difficult to back away and absolve themselves from the responsibility for the decisions that led to where we stand today. The lines are hardening, and across them the confrontation between pro- and antinuclear thinking becomes more truculent and defensive. What has plummeted as costs and accidents have soared is trust. And it is trust that continues to ooze rapidly away as defensive men dissimulate, lie and cover up the failures. We shall have to take a look at this in a mood of saddened resolution.

17 Atomic energy: Dissolving the glue of trust

The soaring costs and numerous accidents in the atomic power industry have produced crises of trust with far-reaching repercussions in the lives of many nations. Trust has eroded because the industry is so massive that few nations have been able to separate the huge economic stakes from the realm of political control in a democratic society – the government itself. In nations traditionally choosing to place the power industry in private hands, the lines of separation have become so blurred that it is often difficult to see where private industry ends and government begins. In countries where matters of national energy are considered government's proper business, the atomic power industry has become a large and self-serving arm of government itself, often a "state within a state." Too often those within the inner state begin by disparaging any view they consider "unscientific," and end by expressing a cynical contempt for democratic government itself. As the director of France's electricity board noted, when asked about bypassing public enquiries. "You don't tell the frogs when you're draining the marsh."

No matter how hard one tries, it is difficult to take a detached and clinical view of the deceit, dissimulation, contempt and lying that so frequently characterize human attitudes, behavior and announcements in these areas. Those still holding a set of ideals about democratic government are either outraged, or brought to the verge of a cynical view that is deadly to democratic forms of life. For those already cynical or fearful towards government the deceit merely deepens and confirms the sense of numb futility. Neither encourage a feeling that democratic forms have, or even deserve, much chance in the future.

If detachment is impossible, then at least outrage is better than a sense of resigned futility. Our first job is to understand how the sense of trust became eroded so quickly, how hopes so bright only 30 years ago became so tarnished. The span of 30 years is significant; it is roughly the time most people take to reach positions of prominence and authority in their professional careers, and they usually reach these levels by dedicating their lives to the careers that brought them to the top. Many start at 25 to build a professional life in industry because it is seen as worthwhile, either for its own sake, or because it makes a lot of money. We commit ourselves, often to a degree that only neglected families realize, and when the industry we have built begins to crumble we sense that we are being destroyed too. Sometimes the job and the self are nearly one and the same. There is nothing unusual about this, but it often takes more courage than most aging men and women have to admit that the young people they once were took a fork in the road that led to a lifelong mistake.

The mistake was not the commitment to peaceful uses of atomic energy, which in the 1950s promised so much, but to decisions taken with so little thought for future safety requirements. As we have seen, these involve two fundamental problems; the control of the light water reactor, and the disposal of the inevitable atomic waste. In that first decade of enthusiasm there were few people capable of reflecting quietly and thinking through the consequences. Government was either scientifically impotent, or equally caught up in the push for power, prestige and an overwhelming greed for huge world markets. Those who counselled governments were themselves the strongest proponents of atomic power. National academies of sciences were asked to advise, and they called upon atomic "experts" in turn who were often part and parcel of the emerging and highly enthusiastic atomic industry. There were few independent voices to be heard. Those who might have been available were either silenced by the relief they felt in turning away from destruction, or were distrusted in an industry that had emerged under great secrecy and heavy security controls during wartime. Again and again that old Latin question "Who guards the guards?" comes to the fore, and if it is not answered the glue of trust will weaken further, and democratic government itself will be put in grave peril. As Leo Tolstoy noted long before atomic energy was born:

> I know that most men – not only those considered clever, but even those who are clever and capable of understanding the most difficult scientific, mathematical, or philosophic problems – can seldom discern even the simplest and most obvious truth if it be such that it obliges them to admit the falsity of conclusions they have formed, perhaps with much difficulty – conclusions of which they are proud, which they have taught the others, and on which they have built their lives.

When you have followed a course that has led to a perilous situation there are only two things you can do. You can admit the mistakes, and examine again the alternative "forks in the road" that you bypassed the first time around, or you can continue to try to justify the forks in the road that led to the present situation. In the face of overwhelming distrust, the first alternative is slowly gaining ground, as we shall see later. The second alternative is still dominant, a stance of obdurate and truculent justification, either on the grounds of "no gas, no oil, no coal, no choice," the slogan of necessity chosen by several national atomic power programs, or by covering up, dissimulating, and, if necessary, lying. The latter is a strategy used *in extremis*, and it is ultimately based on an overweening arrogance that dares the lie to be uncovered, and challenges anyone to do anything about it if it is. It is not a strategy engendering the sense of trust that must ultimately ground democratic government and society itself.

Justification by deceit is a difficult and stressful course for anyone to follow, and perhaps especially for those who have been trained in the physical sciences. Science, as one of the finest of human endeavors, can only be built on trust because by its very nature it is a "building" endeavor. In its larger context it is always a cooperative enterprise. You must be able to trust the work and results of other scientists anywhere in the world. Selecting observations carefully to prove your point, discarding those which question it, or falsifying experimental results are all rightly condemned. Tests may have to be repeated, and results must be confirmed, not because you distrust the moral integrity of the original researcher, but because genuine errors and misinterpretations are always thoroughly human possibilities. Ideally, you go for the ideas not the person. However fashionable the idea of a relative truth may appear at the shallow cocktail party level, *the* truth is still held as an ideal and a touchstone for many scientists. Deceit comes hard.

Equally disturbing as the litany of accidents and coverups in the physical operations of the plants themselves are the attempts to deceive when the consequences lie beyond immediate operations. These are also undertaken on the grounds of increasing or retaining public trust, and three basic strategies have been chosen: the withholding or falsification of epidemiological data; the pseudomathematization of risks; and the corruption of public officials and private citizens, including the falsification of documents.

Health risks are often difficult to establish because the tumors and malignancies of individuals can seldom be ascribed definitively to radiation. To establish reasonable evidence requires the most patient and thoughtful analysis of scrupulously gathered and reported data. Unfortunately, the data are almost always gathered by those who wish to protect the reputation of the atomic industry. In Britain the falsification of medical data by withholding crucial information has become particularly serious, although in general the standards of record keeping are high. A major problem is how to "disconnect" those undertaking the analyses from the nuclear industry itself, and so establish genuine and independent credibility. Like the statisticians hired by the tobacco industry to "prove" that smoking does not cause lung cancer ("It's only correlated with it and correlation is not causation" they chorus), so those in the atomic power industry, or brought in by the industry as consultants from the outside, may find it difficult to blow the whistle. Any consultant who actually demonstrates a health risk is not very likely to be asked to consult again. The result is that those who do establish a significant increase in childhood leukemias around Harwell, England, according to their own statistical methodology, end up by concluding the risk is "not great," and a fivefold increase in childhood cancers around Dounray in Scotland is dismissed as being possibly caused by radioactive discharges. Men exposed to tritium at an experimental UK reactor at Winfrith were found to have nine times the national rate of prostate cancer, and high rates for testicular cancer, but the report concluded that "working in [atomic] establishments carries no significant risk to health." Confidence in such conclusions is not increased when it is learnt that files on people who had died 20 years before had been destroyed, or those recording the health of people who had died after leaving the industry were "accidently withheld."

Other and perfectly legal ploys are also used. A UK national study of plutonium accumulation showed minute quantities in the tracheobronchial lymph nodes (10 mbq), rising to 35 in ordinary people in Cumbria, to 1,600, 4,100 and 73,300 in Sellafield workers. At this point a law stating that it is illegal to examine autopsy tissue except for cause of death began to be enforced more rigorously, but British Nuclear Fuels still conducts such analyses through the NRPB, which is not allowed to reveal the results to the public. One is reminded of the statement of Finland's Minister of Home Affairs, "There is no reason to inform. It will only create anxiety." In one case, when an independent consultant was used by a lobby for Scottish fishing interests, pressure was put on the lobby to stop the consultant from presenting his recommendations against a proposed reprocessing plant discharging into the North Sea. The original criticism of the consultant by a civil servant was never published, nor was it shown to the consultant, who had no chance to reply to the charges.

When the worst comes to the worst, evidence is withheld, or only put forward when it appears likely that it can weaken conclusions unacceptable to the industry and the government. After the Black Report into the Sellafield discharges was published, British Nuclear Fuels admitted it had provided "by mistake" the wrong amounts of uranium discharged in the 1950s. It turned out that 20 kilograms, not half a kilogram, had been released. Similarly, an independent study by the University of Birmingham investigated the cancers of British ex-servicemen who had taken part in atomic bomb tests in Australia. The epidemiologists, including some from the Oxford Childhood Cancer Survey, found a high incidence based on the number of men the Ministry of Defence initially said had taken part. When the results of the analysis showed a statistically significant effect, the Ministry of Defence suddenly increased the number of men it said had taken part, so diluting the analysis with a larger "population" to the point where the results were thrown into doubt. As for a parallel government analysis, it had followed impeccable epidemiological practice by comparing the servicemen exposed to atomic bomb blasts and debris with a control group of similar men matched for age and length of tropical service. Only then could they see if cancer rates for those exposed were statistically significant over and above the control group. By their own methodology they were forced to conclude that there was indeed a significant increase, one very unlikely to have occurred by chance sampling effects. However, their embarrassing scientific conclusions were neatly explained away by saying that their control group had somehow displayed an unusually low incidence. "The difference . . . was largely due to extraordinarily low rates in the controls." If you cannot come up with the approved solution one way, you have to go against all your scientific training and choose another.

Even an official study commissioned by Britain's NRPB raised the question of whether it could trust the Ministry of Defence to provide the correct information, while the former soldiers, who formed the British Nuclear Test Veterans Association, said the official investigation by the NRPB would whitewash everything anyway. Chains of trust dissolve, and with it the glue of confidence that holds a society together. Who trusts whom when the people do not trust an official government body that does not trust an official government body?

Another way to allay public criticism and concern is to confound people with pseudoscientific mathematical computations that show how safe the atomic power industry really is. Here we enter a realm that is the modern equivalent of astrology and fortune-telling, even though this practice is carried out in the name of science by people holding doctoral degrees. It is called "calculating the probability of risk," one of the most outrageous "scientific" deceptions ever foisted on a once-trusting public. In order to quiet public fears, the chances or probabilities of nuclear accidents are computed to be so small that "no one in his right mind" could rationally refuse to go forward.

Unfortunately, there are so many problems with the probabilities computed by the "risk bookies" of the atomic power industry that all credence is lost once they are closely examined. The problem is that most people are not sure how these probabilities are computed, and they are often cowed by the apparent scientific authority of those doing the computing. It is fortunate for them that they seldom have to show where they started or how they arrived at their results. The first problem is that these probabilities can never be put to the test, meaning that they can never be shown to be right or wrong because there is no way anyone can ever confirm or deny them except possibly over many human lifetimes. Even this length of time would assume that the "experimental conditions" of reactor construction and design would remain the same over centuries, and that people would stand around counting the explosions in the year 2400 to see if the estimates of 1970 were "on target." This is a scenario too mad to contemplate.

Secondly, there is absolutely no basis of experience on which to ground such computations. They are all based on blind guesses, assumptions pulled out of thin air which quickly become forgotten as thinking is drawn to the more purposeful task of calculating. One honest computer expert, closely involved with software designed to increase safety, said "this probabilistic approach is not the right way to certify systems. We don't have adequate experience to make claims on the probability. This is psychology, not engineering." Another leading software designer said "it is the specification . . . that turns out to be wrong . . . they should not fail more than once in 100 million reactor years [but] these are orders of magnitude beyond what we can guarantee scientifically . . . nobody is collecting statistically valid data . . . We do not know how bad it is today, so we cannot estimate how bad it will be tomorrow."

To unravel these two points, let us start with more familiar and practical examples. When engineers design bridges they try to take into account the flood waters that the bridges will have to withstand. Often the "100 year flood" is taken as a standard, the maximum flood expected once in a century, and the bridge is designed accordingly, usually with a good dose of rather sensible "fudge factor" to make the bridge even stronger just in case. Most responsible engineers are well aware of the difficulties of estimating the chances of such events, and often increase their estimates to build in an extra margin of safety. Even so, two weeks after a bridge is finished, the "200 year flood" may come along and wipe the new bridge away. Were the probabilities wrong? Possibly, but probably not, although no one can ever tell for sure. But at least the engineers computed the probabilities on the basis of prior experience. That experience consists of the history of floods and all the stream gauge records that they can get their hands on, and the longer the record the better. These concrete and carefully measured values of actual events are used to extrapolate from our current experience to the chance or probability of other events appearing out of the future, and the computations are underpinned by a great deal of thinking incorporated into a Theory of Extreme Events. If you are worried about the occurrence of floods and earthquakes, you do not examine the entrails of a cat, but try to put your hands on the best scientific records available, and hope the future will look something like the past – at least in broad outline.

It is exactly the same in medicine, where doctors may have to estimate the risk of a particular operation. They do it by keeping, collating, and analyzing the outcomes of previous operations, and they use this previous experience as one of many factors to assess the chance of success with a particular patient. Surgery tends to be highly conservative, not simply on good moral grounds, but on scientific grounds as well. The real risk of a new operation is difficult, if not impossible to estimate until it has been tried many times, so that the proportion or chance of success can be grounded on actual experience.

But what about the probabilities computed so confidently for accidents in the atomic power industry? They too can never be tested, so those undertaking these ridiculous computations can never be held to account. Probability is the Pontius Pilate of the scientific world. Only when it is grounded in experience, or based upon a scrupulously derived mathematical theory of large numbers, in which the theoretical conditions are specified with extreme care and rigor, does it have any concrete meaning. Otherwise it is literally meaning-less. As for experience, there was none when the original minute chances were computed and trotted out. In Britain, a report of the Central Electricity Generating Board in 1975 said the chances of a severe reactor accident were one in a million years. No grounds for the probability were put forward, and it most likely represented little more than the wishful thinking of the chairman who strongly endorsed the report. In the United States, the casualties estimated by one "disaster scenario" study of the Nuclear Regulation Commission (NRC) were made public by a congressman two years after TMI. The embarrassed NRC said there was no cause for alarm because it could not really happen. After all, the chances of a reactor failure were 1 in 100,000, the chances of the weather conditions assumed by the scenario were 1 in 10,000, so multiply the two together and the chances of the event occurring were one in a billion. The trouble was that neither of the first two probabilities could be grounded in anything vaguely approaching concrete evidence, and the arithmetic was more appropriate for the gaming tables of a casino regularly fleecing its customers than a careful and thoughtful scientific analysis. Later post-TMI estimates from the United States and West Germany put forward a prediction of one core-damaging accident every 10,000 years, and then an Oakridge report said every 4,000 years. This was followed by an NRC report just before

Chernobyl of one every 3,333 years. Notice how the numbers, like the walls of Joshua's Jericho, come tumbling down.

Where do these probabilities come from? Some try the "reductionist" ploy: you take every nut, bolt, pipe, joint, pump, switch ... every component you can think of, and try to place a probability on it of not failing. Many of these components have never actually had the testing that ordinary household appliances undergo, but numbers are pinned on them nevertheless. You then aggregate them by multiplying them all together to give some equally meaningless probability of failure for the whole. If this is too high, you go back and pin bigger probabilities for non-failure on the components until you come up with something considered acceptable by someone at the top. The problem is that you have to believe what you are doing, and hope others will believe you too. Few do anymore. TMI happened after about 1,500 reactor years of operation, and Chernobyl another 1,900 reactor years later. Playing their own probability game, using one accident every 3,333 years and the roughly 394 reactors in operation now, there would be a 92 percent chance of a major nuclear accident over the next 20 years. Post-Chernobyl calculations by Swedish and West German analysts come up with a 70 percent chance of a severe failure every 5.4 years, or roughly three before the year 2000. As the probability of failure goes up does the price of your children go down?

The third strategy of deceit that erodes public trust is the corruption of those who work in the atomic power industry. Corruption can be found at almost any level and at any stage. In the United States, nuclear plant workers were bribed with sums up to $35,000 by the industry if they would refrain from raising safety issues that would delay the construction of new facilities. This practice was not condemned by the NRC, whose own future was put in doubt in 1989 by a Senate subcommittee probing such scandalous conduct.

Even worse corruption has been found in affiliated industries acquiring and disposing of nuclear materials. In a sense this is only the most serious aspect of the much more general problem of disposing of toxic materials, either chemical or nuclear. Few are willing to accept toxic materials in their own areas, and after a while, as dangerous materials pile up, the solution is often some form of illegal dumping or processing. By definition, criminal elements converge on such problems where large payments or bribes are the norm. Illegal disposal of chemicals is relatively simple: trucks carry them in liquid form and release them along roadsides in rural areas, or dump solid wastes in sites used for household garbage. Usually the bribes are high, but not as high as the cost of legal disposal.

At the moment the risks of getting caught are not great, and the penalties relatively minor.

Radioactive waste is more difficult to handle, and a variety of national laws and international agreements attempt to enforce the strict regulations governing nuclear waste disposal. Kilograms of plutonium may get lost in pipes, but under the Nuclear Nonproliferation Treaty they are not meant to be sold and shipped abroad. Where responsible governments are closely involved in the disposal and reprocessing of radioactive waste it is difficult to cheat too much. Unfortunately, a considerable portion of the waste disposal industry is in private or semi-private hands, and here corruption is much easier. This is not to say that every man has his price. Some do not, no matter what sums of money are involved. It is enough to acknowledge that some men undoubtedly do have their price, and that in a billion dollar industry the prices can go high, quite as high as those reported in the cocaine and drug industry which has also corrupted both government official and private operator.

In West Germany and Belgium the high prices were offered and accepted under circumstances that are still not entirely clear, but with distressing implications both nationally and internationally. Safety officials at West German nuclear plants were bribed to release radioactive waste to a Belgian reprocessing plant, and Belgian officials accepted payment to take the waste and accept the falsified documents. At the same time a major manufacturer of nuclear fuel knew the bribery and falsification was going on, but failed to notify the authorities. The manufacturer has admitted spending $12 million on bribes, and a manager of the disposal company transporting the waste killed himself after police accused him of spending another $9 million more. Two others took their own lives as the scandal unfolded, and the president of the West German state of Hesse, and a Green member of the Belgian Parliament, charged that fissionable materials from the Belgian reprocessing plant had been shipped via Lubeck to Libya and Pakistan. The Belgian firm had helped to build Pakistan's test reactor, which is generally acknowledged to be part of Pakistan's drive to make the atomic bomb.

It is hardly going too far to say that these criminal undertakings by the atomic energy industry have dissolved the last vestiges of trust in West Germany and Belgium and have spread a ripple of increasing distrust throughout Europe. Once again the ultimate consequences are political, and it is important to point towards the role played by a small number of people in the various Green parties around Europe. As in any political group there are variations from the most thoughtful to the most emotional, but it is worth reflecting on the political impact that a relatively small number of people have had on the ethical and moral stance of the political process. As we have already seen in Sweden, polls indicated that the Greens could well form the majority balance in any future coalition, and they actually were the critical weight in a state election in Saxony when the ruling party was thrown out. In West Germany they were one of the major sources producing reliable and accurate information during the first year after Chernobyl, not only for their own countrymen, but also for foreign visitors. There is unquestionably an "international feeling" being generated by people's concern for the planetary environment, a concern that has grasped the fact that political boundaries are no barriers to fallout clouds, acid rain, chemical dumping, and atomic waste disposal. Whatever one feels about the Greens as a political force, few can disparage their moral concern, or fail to sympathize with their call for prudence in the face of industries prepared to pollute the environment to any level they can get away with in their search for cost minimization and profit maximization.

A second political impact has been felt in West Germany itself. In the wake of the damaging disclosures about waste disposal, the Chancellor noted "If the control mechanisms for nuclear materials are not enough, a new system [will be required]." But this means that the Federal government itself will have to become much more involved, and therefore much more closely associated with the industry, a move that in itself carries many political overtones. No political party wants to become associated in people's minds with a corrupt and dangerous industry: the political price at the next election may be too severe. Perhaps environmental concern can keep the flame of democracy burning just a little brighter in an increasingly bureaucratic world. A small number of people can make a difference by reminding those of us who forget that politics without moral concern is tyranny. Edmund Burke once said "It only requires that good men do nothing for tyranny to prevail." The tyrannies of his day took a somewhat different form, but his words force us to reflect upon the tyrannies in our own times.

18 Aristotle's Virtues and inherently safe reactors

If trust has virtually disappeared, is there any hope, any silver lining to the dark Chernobyl cloud? A few things here and there perhaps, a handful of positive pickings from an environmental disaster, but we shall have to stretch our imaginations to glean them. We have witnessed a small forward lurch in the glacial movement of international cooperation, for once the accident at Chernobyl was known it catalyzed the new and unfamiliar policy of *glasnost* that was slowing creaking into action against old and deeply ingrained bureaucratic habits. The Soviet Union eventually became remarkably open and forthright about the accident, and gained the respect of many for this considerable change in policy. Her willingness to report fully to the International Atomic Energy Agency at Vienna, and her declaration to share the unfolding epidemiological knowledge with others in the future, can only reflect credit upon her.

We have also learnt some unexpected things about nature as a result of the fortuitous "experiment." Chernobyl deposited widespread fallout over the oceans, and this acted as a short radioactive pulse moving like a tracer through a complex ecological system. Oceanographers in the Mediterranean were surprised how the fallout pulse deposited on the surface drifted down to the bottom sediments in a few days, rather than in the years predicted by their models. The facts of nature have an astringent and purifying effect upon the model building speculators. The fallout was rapidly consumed by zooplankton feeding on the surface, and they incorporated the radionuclides in their fecal pellets, making up 70 percent of the sediments. In this way the radioactivity was taken out of the food chain much more quickly than expected, although any shrimp or fish feeding on the plankton would amplify the radioactivity drastically during the first week. We have already seen the orders of magnitude effects of such food chain amplification in the Baltic, and we also know from studies in Alaska that whales take up this radioactive "signature" as they lay down layers of baleen. From these we now realize that grievous errors have been made in estimating the age and sexual maturity of the endangered bowhead whale. If we want to date surviving creatures over the next half century we should look for the mark of Chernobyl in tooth and bone. Unfortunately, a sign of international scientific cooperation that ought to be taken for granted, plus bone layers and fecal pellets hardly constitute a positive balance. Is there nothing else?

Perhaps there is. Chernobyl was an event of the physical world generated by the human presence and reflecting back on both the human and living worlds. Suppose Chernobyl had not happened when it did? Would our world be the same today? Not physically, of course, with 2 kilograms of various radionuclides scattered over parts of Sweden alone, but would our human world of caring and concern be the same? Or would we have carried on unreflectively and unthinkingly as before? Perhaps, in some strange way, jolting events from the physical world remind us again of our own humanity, and of our human capacity to reflect, in our own time and place, upon what we are, and upon the responsibilities granted to us. Perhaps Chernobyl will help us take a step along the path of thinking again.

This implies, of course, that we have not been thinking, a notion that will initially outrage many scientists and politicians, most of whom will insist that they have been thinking all along. After all, learning about atomic fission, calculating the requirements for atomic reactors, and computing the probabilities of their success or failure ... surely all these activities require thinking? How could any reasonable person imply that hundreds of thousands of good scientists have not been thinking, and thinking very hard at that?

But it depends on what you mean by thinking. The issue of atomic power is not in its ground a scientific one, just a matter of computing and calculating, and the scientific world is impotent to seek a solution until older and prior claims to thought are met. The primary issues are moral and ethical, and about these science is dumb. We shall have to reach back and more deeply into our tradition to think them again in their own time and place. We find these issues in Aristotle, as the moral virtues of courage (*andreia*) and truthfulness (*aletheia*), and the practical virtue of prudence (*phronesis*), but they are informed by words at the very dawn of our western thinking – *phusis* (nature), *logos* (reason), and *dike* (justice). To think reasonably and justly about nature, in the form of atomic power and energy, is to think reflectively and deliberately away from the realm of science as we know it today. What we call a physical science tries to demonstrate things that are invariable, things that must be of necessity. Hence the striving and seeking towards those regularities we call laws, and the ability they give us to predict from their authoritative mathematical necessity. As Aristotle says on four occasions, "No one deliberates about things that are invariable."

So to be prudent is to deliberate, to reflect, upon things that are variable, that need not be "of necessity." These are not the invariables of nature like halflives of radionuclides and fissionable critical masses, but matters of deliberate human choice. This does not say that those engaged in science cannot be prudent. They can indeed reflect prudently upon certain aspects of their work, but they do so precisely in areas where things are variable and choices can be made, where precautions can be taken, and where judgements touch the moral ground. Is it prudent to undertake genetic engineering? Is it prudent to choose a light water reactor? In reflecting prudently they leave the realm of scientific demonstration of the invariable. The probability of reactor failure, we recall, is not demonstrable, and does not belong to the scientific realm, no matter what the doctoral qualifications of those doing the computing.

The problems of the atomic energy programs are not scientific problems in any strict sense. They are moral problems, and they arise from the apparent difficulty many have of moving from the demonstrating of the inevitable to the deliberation of the variable. Scientific solutions to these problems are sought in areas of human thinking where the answers cannot lie. And to the degree that we cannot, or are unprepared to think in these reflective ways, with prudence informed by a concern for moral good, so we lose our own humanity and become the machines that so many working in the field of artificial intelligence insist we are. Never did we require real intelligence more, that old intelligence of intuition (*nous*). Those whose intuition tells them that we have chosen a maker of energy so dangerous that no prudent person would take such an option are not drawing their conclusion on scientific grounds. And properly so, for those grounds do not, and cannot, contain the answer.

Chernobyl brought us face to face with a dilemma, and if any good may be said to have come from the catastrophe it is the possibility that it has opened the path of reflective thinking once again. The dilemma comes from the fact that it is not easy to think prudently, for the choices are agonizing. We have built a civilization on energy. Our movements, our warmth, our food, our communications, our material comfort . . . all require prodigious amounts of energy, and we have fallen into profligate habits. Even the stability of nations, and therefore the world system made up by them, becomes questionable when energy sources are suddenly placed in jeopardy. If civilization is to continue to unfold in more humane ways, the energy to fulfill the hopes and necessities of civilized life must be there. We must also reflect upon the soaring growth in human populations that provides the ultimate driving engine of energy demand. It is not, despite the simplistic Marxist claims, *just* a matter of redistribution. The sheer pressure of people on energy resources and a fragile environment lies behind this horn of the dilemma.

The other horn is the growing awareness that conventional forms of gas, coal, and oil are limited, and create conditions that even now may be producing global effects not experienced by the planet for millions of years. From ice and sedimentary cores in icecaps and sea bottoms, we can describe the rise and fall of temperatures over the past 400,000 years with great fidelity from ratios of carbon isotopes. There is an almost perfect correlation with the glacial ages, lending great credence to the careful cyclical reconstruction. At this moment, the carbon dioxide discharges accumulating from the industrial and technological revolutions of the nineteenth and twentieth centuries have led us to a height on the rhythmic cycle not seen before in the long record. Some feel intuitively that it would be prudent to bring these discharges and levels down. We are afraid of levels not reached before, of thresholds where system behavior may flip over into another regime. Gaia, like Atlas carrying her, may shrug, but the itch she gets rid of may be the human race.

There are also, and inevitably, human costs involved, as those who chose the lightwater reactor so properly point out as they count the number of coal miners killed, the number of train workers maimed. You can compute the tons of coal, the cubic feet of gas, per human being lost, the number of fingers, hands, and silicon-wracked lungs per erg of energy. There is no question that a safer form of energy generation is needed. The problem is that once thinking goes down that calculative track it never reflects and asks whether there was a better path worth taking, whether there was another fork in the road where a more prudent choice might have been made. Choices, informed by Aristotle's vices of rashness (*thrasutes*), ambition (*philotimia*), and prodigality (*asotia*), were made, and then reinforced by a generation of men spending material resources beyond the dreams of Midas. Few can be expected now to act with prudence and wisdom with all that inertia of historical investment. If there is a vestige of rational democratic government left, decisions in the future must be taken from their hands.

But the dilemma remains, and dilemmas can only be broken by asking whether the choices giving rise to them are inevitable. It is my contention that they are not. There was a fork in the road not taken, and down that alternative technological path there was a form of atomic energy so safe that even a prudent person might reflect upon it and perhaps choose it. What we require is a form of energy that is inherently safe. Ironically, or perhaps better, tragically, it has been with us for over two decades. It is not a wild-eyed scheme or pipe-dream, but an existing reality for which a well-tested experimental form has been in existence since 1966. Let us see what is involved.

In discussing safety it is useful to think in terms of four levels or possibilities. The first level, virtually unachievable, is a power source presenting no hazard whatsoever. Even coal and gas burning plants can have accidents, even modern wind machines can fracture a stressed blade that kills someone passing by, even a red hot wood-burning stove can injure a child accidentally falling against it. At this level it is not difficult to acknowledge that all sources of power present some hazard, no matter how small. But at the next level up we might think of designing power sources that are inherently safe, by which we mean that they do not require any active intervention if anything should go wrong, and that they are generally immune to human errors and structural failures. In brief, if something should go wrong, then the power source will shut itself down, or reach a stable state with no dangerous consequences, simply "through the laws of physics," those Aristotelian statements about the "invariable." At the third level we might have a power source that needs no active intervention when something goes awry, but which is not immune to operator error, or to major structural failure. Given the constant input of human error to every accident and major emergency shutdown this is hardly a desirable design standard. Finally, and the fourth and most dangerous level of all, are those power generating systems that definitely require some sort of positive corrective responses to parts failing or to human error. These "worst scenario" systems are not immune to major structural failure, and they require backup systems of backup systems to somehow achieve defense in depth.

The latter, of course, is what was chosen; the "worst-scenario," most dangerous, most "complex and unforgiving" system at the level of highest danger – the light water reactor. Given this historical human choice, is it really irrelevant, just a piece of academic pretension, to invoke the Aristotelian virtue of prudence informed by the voice of reason? Clearly, and all our experience of the past 30 years bears it out, the choice of a level four power source was the very worst that could have been made. Was there an alternative? Perhaps at level three, and preferably at that inherently safe design of level two? There are two sorts of reactors at level three, but the operational complexities make them expensive and far beyond the reach of commercial power costs. But what also exists is a design at level two, the inherently safe level, and it is clearly commercially feasible if people are willing to "untrap" their thinking from the years of light water operations.

The inherently or passively safe reactor is called a modular gas cooled reactor or MGR, and it is quite extraordinarily simple compared to the systems now in operation. It consists essentially of a cylinder containing fuel through which the inert gas helium is pumped to cool the fuel and to carry away the heat. This is then used in conventional ways to turn turbines and generate electrical energy. "Yes," says the skeptic, "But what happens when the pumps forcing the helium gas through the fuel fail, and the backup systems fail, and the fuel melts down?" The answer is that it does not, and it cannot, and the secret is in the fuel. This consists of what the German designers call "kernels" or "grains" of uranium dioxide only 0.4 millimeters in diameter, surrounded by four layers of "packaging materials." The first is graphite, the second an extremely hard and dense form of carbon called pyrolytic carbon, the third almost diamond-hard silicon carbide, and the fourth more pyrolytic carbon. One tiny grain is only a millimeter (about 1/40 of an inch) in diameter, and 10–20,000 of these are packed for ease of handling into carbon spheres, or "pebbles," about as big as a billiard ball. Put enough of these billiard balls in a cylinder and they can become a critical mass generating large amounts of heat, but with lots of gaps between the spheres to allow a cooling and heat-carrying gas to pass through. Normally the operating temperature would be about 850° C (1,600° F), mainly because this would allow the use of quite conventional and well-tested turbines. If the gas flow stopped for any reason to create the "worst scenario" then the pebbles would heat to 1,600° C, far below the 2,000° C or more at which the billiard balls of fuel would leak. So there the reactor would sit, the extra heat being carried away by natural thermal radiation and the thermal convection of the air, until someone fixed the pump, patched up the leak releasing inert helium, or connected a new turbine generator to replace the one that had gone wrong. No panic, no particular hurry. The billiard balls just sit there.

Commercially feasible? Yes. A small research MGR has been operating for nearly a quarter of a century at 50 megawatts (MW), too small for commercial operation, but an excellent model for scaling up to 200 MW, at which point it is quite definitely a feasible commercial proposition. This seems much smaller than the recent 3,000 MW light water reactors, those straining for economies of scale that only produce huge and uneconomical overruns, but that is where the "modular" of the MGRs name comes in. The 200 MW output is a *physical* limit set by the diameter of the container to about 3 meters to prevent the innermost billiard balls of fuel becoming too hot if the cooling gas stops flowing. Which is the whole point of course. But you can have one, two, three . . . modules, as many as you like, to produce whatever power you need, and you can scale things up easily as power demand increases, instead of investing billions in one shot to produce excess capacity – like France today. You can also license the MGRs like airplanes by testing them first. No one would trust an airliner that had just rolled off the production line and put it into service without a test flight or two. Why should anyone trust an atomic reactor that cannot pass the inherently safe test? And recall – *trust* is the issue now, not unverifiable and nonsensical pseudoprobabilities.

So can *nothing* go wrong? Are we not tempting the gods after all with our hubris? What about that graphite? It was the cause of Chernobyl's fire, so why head down that path again? There are two answers. First, immense heat is required to ignite graphite, a measure of the extraordinary temperatures experienced in those first seconds of the explosion at Chernobyl. The pyrolytic carbon used in encapsulating the grains in an MGR will not ignite even if an oxyacetylene torch is played on it for half an hour, and these temperatures are more than a thousand degrees hotter than it is physically possible to achieve in the cylinder itself. Secondly, the MGR could be built underground so atmospheric oxygen could be totally excluded. Of course, scaling a 50 MW model up four times requires immense care and knowledge. With over a quarter of a million fresh and partly used pebbles, could a "hot spot" somehow develop by a trillion to one chance? Fortunately, supercomputers can simulate the sorts of random movements and mixings that the pebbles might undergo, and we now know that such hot spots could not occur with the designs available.

But one worry remains: how do you dispose of the spent fuel? Here is still the greatest unresolved problem of all, unresolved by the democratic political process that must make the final decision of acceptability. Let us at least reflect upon the problem by starting at the origin. How are the uranium dioxide grains created before they are given their four coats? Ores relatively rich in uranium are taken from earth and the minute and highly dispersed amounts of fissionable uranium 235 are concentrated by mechanical and chemical means. Fuel creation is a process of concentration, of taking something widely dispersed by nature and bringing it together. So why not think of fuel disposal as the exact opposite, as a process of dispersal, of giving back to nature that which nature gave, but giving it back in such a widely dispersed and dilute form that it presents no danger to life on earth?

In a sense, the fuel for the MGR is already packaged for wide, and highly dilute dispersal. There is the possibility that spent billiard balls could be crushed to release the grains, and these minute and highly stable spheres of 1 millimeter could be slowly broadcast in highly dilute swaths from ships whose release rates and tracks were carefully controlled by the IAEA. The tiny spheres would sink quickly (their density is high compared to sea water), and in a widely dispersed pattern to the deepest parts of the ocean. Here they would sink into the ooze and be covered quickly by the continual rain of particles making the sediments. No ingestion by plankton on the way down – a plankton is much smaller than a pellet and could not ingest anything so many times its size – so there would be no entry point into the food chain. Perhaps inherently safe atomic power is feasible after all.

And so the last swirling effects of that Chernobyl cloud are in human thought itself. The disturbance they create there is just as worrisome, just as difficult as the disturbances in the physical and living worlds that were eventually transmitted to the human structures making up the pieces of our collective human presence. We have seen what effects they have created there too, most of them not commendable, not standing for the best that is in us. But when we trace these effects finally to human thought we stand at the center, and it is from this center that thinking, in its truest, most deliberate and reflective sense, must flow. From out of nature may come the catastrophes of fire, earthquake, wind, flood, and pestilence. Little, if any, human choice is involved. We can only be humble in the face of such events, and try to soften the worst effects and comfort those afflicted by them. But the catastrophe of Chernobyl, standing for atomic power, represents a choice, a genuine human choice to be exercised in the constantly unfolding story that has been given to us. The choice is ours. It is up to us.

Appendix I: Computing energies and doses

Most of the numbers involved boil down to a matter of getting some good operational definitions. We know already (see Chapter 7, How do we measure radiation?) that 1 becquerel is roughly:

$$8 \text{ MeV (from alpha particles)}$$
$$4 \text{ MeV (from beta particles)}$$
$$\text{and } 3 \text{ MeV (from gamma radiation)}$$

to make a total of 15 MeV.

Physicists tell us that:

$$1 \text{ MeV is the same as } 1.6 \times 10^{-6} \text{ ergs, so:}$$
$$1 \text{ becquerel} = 15 \times 1.6 \times 10^{-6} = 24 \times 10^{-6} \text{ ergs.}$$

An absorbed dose (measured in grays) is the amount of energy (ergs) absorbed by a unit mass (grams) of matter (muscle, bones, cells, etc.)

$$10,000 \text{ ergs per gram} = 1 \text{ gray}$$
$$1 \text{ gray}/100 = 1 \text{ rad}$$

An absorbed dose equivalent (measured in sieverts) weights the different alpha, beta, and gamma energies as follows:

alpha	$8 \text{ MeV} \times 20 =$	160 MeV
beta	$4 \text{ MeV} \times 1 =$	4 MeV
gamma	$3 \text{ MeV} \times 1 =$	3 Mev

to make a total of 167 MeV dose equivalent energy.

This means the absorbed dose of 1 gray, or 10,000 ergs per gram, now becomes:

$$167/15 \times 10,000 = 111,333 \text{ ergs per gram}$$

in terms of absorbed dose equivalent. In other words 1 gray is roughly the same as 11.13 sieverts.

Bibliography

"Acid Soils are Harbouring Chernobyl's Caesium," *New Scientist*, July 16, 1987.

Ahearne, J., "Nuclear Power After Chernobyl," *Science*, vol. 236, 1987.

Alexandropoulos, N. et al., "Chernobyl Fallout on Ionnina, Greece," *Nature*, 322, 1986.

"Amber Light for Nuclear Power," *Nature*, vol. 325, 1987.

Amerisov, A., "A Chronology of Soviet Media Coverage," *Bulletin of the Atomic Scientists*, vol. 43, 1986.

ApSimon, H. and J. Wilson, "Tracking the Cloud from Chernobyl," *New Scientist*, July 17, 1986.

Aristotle, *The Nicomachean Ethics* (Harmondsworth: Penguin Books, 1976).

Atkin, R., "A Theory of Surprises," *Environment and Planning B*, vol. 1981.

Barnaby, F., "Chernobyl: The Consequences in Europe," *Ambio*, vol. 15, 1986.

Beresford, N. et al., *A Comparison of 1986 and 1987 Caesium Activities of Vegetation in the Restricted Area of North Wales* (Grange-over-Sands, Cumbria: Institute of Terrestrial Ecology, 1987).

Bohlen, C., "Kiev, Its Playground Vacant, Scrubs On," *Washington Post*, June 9, 1986.

Bohlen, C. and W. Pincus, "Anatomy of an Accident: A Logistical Nightmare," *Washington Post*, October 26, 1986.

Broad, W., "Rise in Retarded Children Predicted from Chernobyl," *New York Times*, February 16, 1987.

Bunyard, P., "The Sellafield Discharges," *The Ecologist*, vol. 16, 1986.

Bunyard, P. and G. Searle, "The Effects of Low-Dose Radiation," *The Ecologist*, vol. 16, 1986.

Bureau Européen des Unions de Consommateurs, *Chernobyl: The Aftermath* (Brussels: BEUC, 1986).

"Chernobyl Babies," *New Scientist*, vol. 236, 1987, p. 22.

"Chernobyl Bone-marrow Transplants 'were a failure'," *New Scientist*, September 4, 1986.

"Chernobyl Cleanup Products," *Engineering News Record*, June 5, 1986.

Chernobyl: Its Impact on Sweden (Stockholm: National Institute of Radiation Protection, 1986).

"Chernobyl: UK Government Accused of Complacency," *WISE News Communique*, vol. 254, 1986, pp. 5–6 (Amsterdam: World International Science on Energy).

"Cleaning Nuclear Steam Generators," *e-lab: Current Research at the Energy Laboratory*, October–December 1986 (Cambridge, Massachusetts: Massachusetts Institute of Technology).

"Commission Cautions Over Caesium Levels in Food," *New Scientist*, May 28, 1987.

Connor, S., "Protein Reveals Damage from Radiation," *New Scientist*, January 14, 1988.

Connor, S., "Risk and the Radioactive Science," *New Scientist*, February 4, 1988.

"Crystal Detector Gives Britain a Map of Chernobyl's Fallout," *New Scientist*, February 25, 1989.

"Czech Authorities Round Up Outspoken Scientists," *New Scientist*, November 26, 1987.

"Czechs Come Clean Over Reactor Faults," *New Scientist*, June 4, 1987.

Dear, M. and J. Wolch, *Landscapes of Despair* (Princeton: Princeton University Press, 1987).

Diehl, J., "Chernobyl's Other Losses," *The Washington Post*, June 8, 1986.

Diehl, J., "East Bloc to Push Nuclear Power," *Washington Post*, November 6, 1986.

Douglas, M., *Risk Assessment According to the Social Sciences* (Andover, Hants: Routledge and Kegan Paul, 1986).

Dyring, E., "Sweden After Chernobyl: Revival of the Nuclear Power Debate," *Current Sweden*, no. 354, 1987 (Swedish Institute).

Edin, K. A., "Sweden After Chernobyl: Consequences of the Nuclear Accident," *Current Sweden*, no. 353, 1987 (Swedish Institute).

Edwards, M., "Chernobyl – One Year After," *National Geographic Magazine*, vol. 171, 1987.

"Estimating Potential Releases," *e-lab: Current research in the Energy Labortory*, October–December 1986 (Cambridge, Massachusetts: Massachusetts Institute of Technology).

Falioner, I., "^{131}I in Ruminant Thyroids after Nuclear Releases," *Nature*, 322, 1986.

Ferriman, A. and R. McKie, "Blunder Puts Children in Cancer Peril," *Observer*, September 21, 1986.

Findahl, O. and I. Lindblad, *Forty Days with Chernobyl News on Radio and Television* (Stockholm: Sveriges Radio, 1988).

Flavin, C., *Reassessing Nuclear Power: The Fallout from Chernobyl* (Washington, DC: Worldwatch Institute, 1987).

Fouguet, D., "West European Nations Under Fire for Their Reaction to Chernobyl," *Christian Science Monitor*, August 6, 1986.

Gale, R., "Chernobyl: Biomedical Consequences," *Issues in Science and Technology*, vol. 3, 1986.

Gamlin, L., "Sweden's Factory Forests," *New Scientist*, January 28, 1988.

Gofman, J. *Assessing Chernobyl's Cancer Consequences: Application of Four 'Laws' of Radiation Carcinogenesis* (Berkeley: University of California, Department of Biophysics and Medical Physics, 1986).

Gofman, J., "Warning from the A-bomb Study about Low Radiation Exposures," *Health Physics*, 56, 1989.

Goldman, M. et al., *Assessment of the Dosimetric and Health Implications of the*

Chernobyl Reactor Accident (Washington, DC: Office of Environmental Health and Environmental Research, United States Department of Energy, 1986).

Gubaryev, V., *Sarcophagus* (Harmondsworth: Penguin Books, 1987).

Hall, E., *Radiation and Life* (Oxford: Pergamon Press, 1984).

Hall, E., *Nuclear Politics: The History of Nuclear Power in Britain* (Harmondsworth: Penguin Books, 1986).

Hamman, H. and S. Parrott, *Mayday at Chernobyl* (London: Hodder and Stoughton, 1987).

Hawkes, N. et al., *Chernobyl: The End of the Nuclear Dream* (New York: Vintage Books, 1987).

Hecht, J., "Living with Low-level Hazards," *New Scientist*, July 23, 1987.

Heidegger, M., *A Question Concerning Technology* (New York: Harper and Row, 1977).

Hohenemser, C., "The Accident at Chernobyl: Health and Environmental Consequences and the Implications for Risk Management," *Annual Review of Energy*, 13, 1988.

Hohenemser, C. and O. Renn, "Chernobyl's Other Legacy," *Environment*, vol. 3, 1988.

Hohenemser, C. et al., "Chernobyl: An Early Report," *Environment*, 28, 1986.

Horrill, A., *Chernobyl Fallout in Great Britain* (London: National Environmental Research Council, 1987).

Horrill, A. and B. Howard, "Problems Encountered in Obtaining Realistic Radionuclide Transfer Factors for Sheep," in *Seminar on the Environmental Transfer to Man of Radionuclides Released from Nuclear Installations* (Vienna: International Atomic Energy Agency, 1984).

Howard, B., "Aspects of the Uptake of Radionuclides by Sheep Grazing on an Estuarine Saltmarsh. 1. The Influence of Grazing Behavior and Environmental Variability on Daily Intake," *Journal of Environmental Radioactivity*, vol. 3, 1985.

Howard, B. "^{137}Cs Uptake by Sheep Grazing Tidally-inundated and Inland Pastures Near the Sellafield Reprocessing Plant," in Coughtrey, P. et al., (eds), *Pollutant Transport and Fate in Ecosystems* (Oxford: Blackwell Scientific Protection, vol. 7, 1987.

Howard, B. and D. Lindley, "Aspects of the Uptake of Radionuclides by Sheep Grazing on an Estuarine Saltmarsh. 2. Radionuclides in Sheep Tissues," *Journal of Environmental Radioactivity*, vol. 3, 1985.

Howard, B. and F. Livens, "May Sheep Safely Graze?," *New Scientist*, April 23, 1987.

Howard, B. et al., "A Comparison of Caesium Activity in Sheep Remaining on Upland Areas Contaminated by Chernobyl Fallout with Those Removed to Less Active Lowland Pasture," *Journal of the Society for Radiation Protection*, vol. 7, 1987.

Hughes, J. and G. Roberts, *The Radiation Exposure of the UK Population* (London: Her Majesty's Stationery Office, 1984).

Imbrie, J., "A Theoretical Framework for the Pleistocene Iceages," *Journal of the*

Geological Society of London, vol. 142, 1985.

Interim Report on Fallout Situation in Finland from April 26 to May 9 (Helsinki: Finnish Center for Radiation and Nuclear Safety, 1986).

International Atomic Energy Agency, *The International Nuclear Safety Advisory Group Summary Report on the Post-Accident Review Meeting on the Chernobyl Accident* (Vienna: IAEA, 1986).

International Commission on Radiological Protection, *Evaluation of Radiation Doses to Body Tissues from Internal Contamination Due to Occupational Exposure* (Oxford: Pergamon Press, 1965).

International Commission on Radiological Protection, *Limits for Intakes of Radionuclides by Workers* (Oxford: Pergamon Press, 1978).

"Is Cumbria Sheep Ban a Sellafield Cover-up?" *Farmer's Weekly*, July 4, 1986.

Jacobs, Brian, "The Politics of Radiation," *Greenpeace*, August 1988.

Jaworowski, Z., "Chernobyl Accident: Emergency Monitoring and Protection Measures in Poland," Report of the Central Laboratory for Radiological Protection, Warsaw, November 1986.

Jensen, M. and J-C Lindhé, *Activities of the Swedish Authorities Following the Fallout from the Soviet Chernobyl Reactor Accident* (Stockholm: National Institute of Radiation Protection).

Jones, R. and R. Southwood (eds), *Radiation and Health* (New York: John Wiley and Sons, 1981).

Kaufman, M., "Three Weeks Later 'The Cloud' Still Bothers the Poles," *New York Times*, May 20, 1986.

Kelly, J., "The Purpose of Project Chariot," *Nuclear Information*, vol. 3, 1961.

Klimov, A., *Nuclear Physics and Nuclear Reactors* (Moscow: Mir Publishers, 1975).

Kjelle, P-E., *Fallout in Sweden from Chernobyl* (Stockholm: National Institute of Radiation Protection, 1986).

Kneale, G. et al., "Hanford Radiation Study III: A Cohort Study of the Cancer Risks from Radiation to Workers at Hanford (1944–77). Deaths by the Method of Regression Models in Life-tables," *British Journal of Industrial Medicine*, vol. 38, 1981.

Kneale, G. et al., "Job Related Mortality Risks of Hanford Workers and Their Relation to Cancer Effects of Measured Doses of External Radiation," *British Journal of Industrial Medicine*, vol. 41, 1984.

Kovalevska, L., "Time Is Not a Private Affair," *Literturna Ukraina*, March 27, 1986.

Laughton, A. et al., *The Disposal of Long-lived and Highly Radioactive Wastes* (London: Cambridge University Press, 1987).

Lee, G., "Chernobyl Evacuees Long for Homes They Left Behind," *Washington Post*, December 14, 1986.

Lester, R., "Rethinking Nuclear Power," *Scientific American*, vol. 254, 1986.

Lidsky, L., "Modular Gas-cooled Reactors for Electric Power Generation," *International Nuclear Engineering Symposium*, Tokai University, Japan, 1986.

Lidsky, L., "Same Nuclear Power," *The New Republic*, December 28, 1987.

Lidsky, L., "Nuclear Power: Levels of Safety," *Radiation Research*, vol. 7, 1988.

Lovelock, J., *Gaia* (London: Oxford University Press, 1979).

Lowry, D., "Corrupt to the Core," *Environment Now*, August 1988.

McCally, M., "Hospital Number Six: A First-Hand Report," *Bulletin of the Atomic Scientist*, 43, 1986.

Macgill, S., *The Politics of Anxiety: Sellafield's Cancer-link Controversy* (London: Pion, 1987).

MacKenzie, D., "Corruption Fuels Radiation Scandal," *New Scientist*, January 14, 1988.

MacKenzie, D., "German Nuclear Scandal Deepens," *New Scientist*, January 21, 1988.

Markham, J., "Estonians Resist Chernobyl Duty," *New York Times*, August 27, 1986.

Marples, D., *Chernobyl and Nuclear Power in the USSR* (New York: St Martin's Press, 1986).

Marples, D., "Chernobyl's Area Declared Unfit for Permanent Habitation," *Report on the USSR*, vol. 1, 1988.

Mascanzoni, D., *The Aftermath of Chernobyl in Sweden: Levels of ^{137}Cs in Foodstuffs* (Uppsala: Swedish University of Agricultural Sciences, 1986).

Meisler, S., "Paris Backtracks on Radiation," *Los Angeles Times*, May 13, 1986.

Miller, J., "Trying to Quell a Furor France Forms a Panel on Chernobyl," *New York Times*, May 14, 1986.

Milne, R., "Is This the End of the Line for Sellafield?," *New Scientist*, February 27, 1986.

Milne, R., "Disastrous Plans for Nuclear Accidents," *New Scientist*, April 23, 1987.

Milne, R., "Lessons for the Soviets," *New Scientist*, April 23, 1987.

Milne, R., "Nuclear Industry Considers Tougher Standards," *New Scientist*, September 3, 1987.

Milne, R., "Computerized Safety Could Be Sizewell's Achilles Heel," *New Scientist*, October 29, 1987.

Milne, R., "Radiation Watchdog Seeks Lower Dose Limit," *New Scientist*, September 3, 1987.

Milne, R., "Chernobyl Disaster Zone to Become National Park," *New Scientist*, no. 1630, 1988.

National Academy of Sciences, *Biological Effects of Ionizing Radiation* (Washington, DC: National Academy of Sciences, 1980).

National Radiological Protection Board, *Living With Radiation* (London: Her Majesty's Stationery Office, 1987).

Neffe, J., "Weizsacker Changes His Mind," *Nature*, vol. 320, 1986.

Nuclear Regulatory Commission, *Reactor Safety Study* (Washington, DC: Nuclear Regulatory Commission, 1975).

Openshaw, S. et al., *Building a Mark I Geographical Analysis Machine for the Automated Analysis of Point Pattern Cancer and Other Spatial Data* (Newcastle upon Tyne: Northern Regional Research Laboratory Report, no. 12, 1987).

Otway, H. and R. Misenta, "Some Human Performance Paradoxes of Nuclear Performance," *Futures*, October 1980.

"PCBs Poison Seals in the North Sea," *New Scientist*, December 11, 1986.

Pentreath, R., *Nuclear Power, Man and the Environment* (London: Taylor and Francis, 1980).

Perrow, C., *Normal Accidents: Living With High-risk Technologies* (New York: Basic Books, 1986).

Persson, C., H. Rodhe and L. DeGeer, "The Chernobyl Accident: A Meteorological Analysis of How Radionuclides Reached and Were Deposited in Sweden," *Ambio*, vol. 16, 1987.

Peterson, R., Lander, L. and H. Blanck, "Assessment of the Impact of the Chernobyl Reactor Accident on the Biota of Swedish Streams and Lakes," *Ambio*, vol. 15, 1986.

Pheasant, S., "The Zeebrugge–Harrisburg Syndrome," *New Scientist*, January 21, 1988.

Pietila, A., "Anxious Kiev Residents Try to Flee by Thousands," *The Sun*, May 8, 1986.

"Radiating Complacency," *The Economist*, September 12, 1987.

"Radiation Dosage: The Legacy of the A-bombs," *The Economist*, September 12, 1987.

"Radiation Dose Figures 'Flawed'," *New Scientist*, September 3, 1987.

"Radiation Test Call for People," *Caern and Denbigh Herald*, August 14, 1987.

Randolph, M. and F. O'Donnell, "When Is a Dose Not a Dose?," *Health Physics*, vol. 50, 1986.

Rich, V., "Byelorussia Still Alarmed by the Effects of Chernobyl Fallout," *Nature*, vol. 337, 1989.

Reactor Accident at Chernobyl, USSR: Radiation Measurements in Denmark, The (Copenhagen: National Agency of Environmental Protection, 1986).

"Recalculating the Cost of Chernobyl," *Science*, vol. 236, 1987.

Rotblat, J., *The Medical Implications of Nuclear War* (Washington, DC: National Academy of Sciences, 1986).

Rotblat, J., "A Tale of Two Cities," *New Scientist*, January 7, 1988.

Salter, M., "Italy: Living with Fallout," *The Atlantic*, January 1987.

Scheer, R., "Chernobyl: Still Far from Normal," *The Seattle Times*, April 26, 1987.

Schelenz, R. and A. Abdel-Rassoul, "Report from Spibersdorf: Post-accident and Radiological Measurements," *International Atomic Energy Agency Bulletin*, Autumn 1986.

Schmemann, S., "Chernobyl Fallout: Apocalyptic Tale and Fear," *New York Times*, July 26, 1986.

Shanker, E., "Soviets Try to Put Lid on Chernobyl Controversy," *Chicago Tribune*, December 19, 1986.

"Sheepish About Calcium," *New Scientist*, August 20, 1987.

"Site for Nuclear Waste Goes West," *New Scientist*, February 26, 1987.

Smith, F. and M. Clark, "Radionuclide Deposition for the Chernobyl Cloud," *Nature*, 322, August 21, 1986.

Snitis, J., *Consequences in Sweden of the Chernobyl Fallout* (Stockholm: National Institute of Radiation Protection, 1986).

"Soviet Union 'showed the world how to evacuate'," *New Scientist*, September 4, 1986.

"Soviets Face Nightmare of Logistics," *Washington Post*, September 26, 1986.

Spiess, F., *Radioisotopes in the Human Body* (New York: Academic Press, 1968).

Stein, R., "Radiation Found in Children," *Washington Post*, December 25, 1986.

Stewart, A., "Delayed Effects of A-bomb Radiation: A Review of Mortality Rates and Risk Estimates for Five-year Survivors," *Journal of Epidemiology and Community Health*, vol. 36, 1982.

Stewart, A., "Detection of Late Effects of Ionizing Radiation: Why Deaths of A-Bomb Survivors Are So Misleading," *International Journal of Epidemiology*, vol. 14, 1985.

Strasser, S., "Kiev's Chernobyl Blues," *Newsweek*, June 16, 1986.

Sumerling, E. et al., "The Transfer of Strontium 90 and Caesium 137 to Milk in a Dairy Herd Grazing Near a Major Nuclear Installation," *Science of the Total Environment*, vol. 34, 1984.

Tiovonen, H. et al., "Aerosols from Chernobyl: Particle Characteristics and Health Implications," *Bergbau und Industriemuseum Theuern*, vol. 16, 1988, pp. 97–105.

The Tolerability of Risk from Nuclear Power Stations (London: Her Majesty's Stationery Office, 1988).

Tucker, A., "The New Chain Metals," *Guardian*, April 26, 1988.

United States Nuclear Regulatory Commission, *Report on the Accident at the Chernobyl Nuclear Power Station*. (Washington, DC: Government Printing Office, 1986).

van den Hock, J., "Caesium Metabolism in Sheep and the Influence of Orally Ingested Bentonite on Caesium Absorbtion and Metabolism," *Zeitschrift für Tierephysologie Tierernahrung und Futtermitterkunde*, vol. 37, 1976.

Wakabayashi, E. et al., "Studies of the Mortality of A-bomb Survivors: Incidence of Cancer in 1959–1978 Based on Tumor Registry, Nagasaki," *Radiation Research*, vol. 93, 1983.

Walker, M., "Two Elderly Women Evade Exodus from Chernobyl," *Manchester Guardian*, June 11, 1986.

Watts, S., "Software Row Dogs Nuclear Power Plans," *New Scientist*, April 1, 1989.

Weaver, D., "How Ministers Misled Britain About Chernobyl," *New Scientist*, October 9, 1986.

Wilson, R., "A Visit to Chernobyl," *Science*, vol. 236, 1987.

World Health Organization (WHO), *Report of Consultation, 6 May 1986 (Provisional)* (Copenhagen: World Health Organization, 1986).

World Health Organization (WHO), *Summary Review of Measurement Results Relevant for Dose Assessment, Update Revision No. 7* (Copenhagen: World Health Organization, 1986).

World Health Organization, *Working Group on Assessment of Radiation Dose Commitment in Europe due to the Chernobyl Accident* (Bilthoren: WHO Regional Office for Europe, 1986).

Wynne, B., "Sheepfarming After Chernobyl," *Environment*, vol. 31, 1989.

Index